I WOKE UP
BLACK

WHAT MY EYES HAVE SEEN, MY EARS HAVE HEARD, AND MY HEART HAS FELT.

Marvin Michael O'Bryant

S.H.E. PUBLISHING, LLC

I WOKE UP BLACK
What My Eyes Have Seen,
My Ears Have Heard,
and My Heart Has Felt

For information contact: info@shepublishingllc.com or visit www.shepublishingllc.com

Cover and Title Page Design by Michelle Phillips of CHELLD3 3D VISUALIZATION AND DESIGN

ISBN: 978-1-953163-81-3

Second Edition: August 2024

10 9 8 7 6 5 4 3 2 1

FOREWARNING

This book speaks about racism, and the perspectives shared are based on the author's personal experiences and understanding. The intent of this book is not to offend or discriminate against any individual or group. The author firmly believes in promoting equality, respect, and empathy for all, regardless of race, ethnicity, or background. He aims to foster open dialogue, encourage self-reflection, and advocate for a more inclusive and harmonious society. It is crucial to approach such a sensitive topic of racism with compassion and a willingness to learn from one another, as we work towards a world free from prejudice and discrimination.

CONTENTS

THIS COUNTRY WAS BUILT

ON THE BACKS OF BLACK PEOPLE

THE CONTRIBUTIONS of our ancestors are evident in the infrastructure we see today: the freeways, railroads, open fields, and surface roads were built by their hands. They toiled in the cotton fields, picking fruits and vegetables, while also taking care of Caucasian children, cooking, and cleaning. In the face of discrimination, black entertainers persevered, putting on shows wherever they could, despite being denied proper accommodation or sleeping arrangements. If you delve into history books, you'll discover the numerous inventions that black individuals have pioneered throughout time, such as the backup light and signal, among many others.

The dynamics within the black family have changed. In the past, borrowing sugar or eggs from a neighbor would pass without much notice, but nowadays, such actions can lead to gossip and judgments within the community. When we move into well-established neighborhoods, we find ourselves compelled to join Neighborhood Watch programs, often requiring substantial monthly fees. Yet, during my upbringing, our neighborhood watch consisted of individuals like Ms. Mayola or Ms. Green, who sat on their front porches, observing everything happening around them. If they caught us doing something wrong, they would call us over, reprimand us, and promise to inform our mothers and grandmothers upon their return.

I recall a friend's remark that struck a chord: the term "hood" for black neighborhoods now symbolizes the absence of neighbors who have moved away, leaving behind a sense of desolation. There was a time when visiting uncles and aunts overnight was a casual affair, but now we must seek permission. Times have indeed changed. Despite the challenges and shifts, there is nothing quite like the joyous moments we experience as black people. Whether it's Thanksgiving, Christmas, New Year's Day, birthdays, barbecues, or family reunions, there is an unparalleled sense of fun in a black person's home. Engaging in activities like playing checkers, monopoly, or jumping rope during family time allows us to temporarily escape our troubles and simply enjoy the company of loved ones.

BLACK HISTORY

I'll be the first to say that I am embarrassed about what I know about our black history. There is way more than just Martin Luther King, Harriet Tubman, and Frederick Douglas. Many black people tried to help us learn about the four hundred years of slavery, and now, in the year 2023, Governor Abbott and his crew of believers have cut out history in the state of Texas. Laws are being made to cut out history. We need to know our history. We need to know about our past. And we need to continue to make history. When our history is not told, it's because people are trying to change our mindset. They want us to believe what they want us to believe about how we were treated and where we came from. It is so sad that some kids won't open a book and learn about our history. Now, the information is available for them to learn the truth. I thank God for the people that stood up and tried to help our people. Their fight helped to change laws; may they rest in peace. Society has allowed the black man to endure years and years of disrespect, abuse, rape, being lied on, overpower, and totally devalue them as nothing. That is enough on a race for four hundred years to cause low esteem, depression, heart aches, pain, tears, and frustration. This is why blacks stay on the edge because we are like a pipe about to burst, so when any Caucasian person, particularly those in leadership, chooses to come with smiles and tricks, we reject it because we have played those games for too long.

For those who still haven't understood, Europeans are not from America, they came here. Blacks are not from America; we were brought here against our will for over four hundred years. We have been here; we have the right to stay here just like everyone else. In my opinion, I think we are one of the most resilient races on the planet. We can survive with nothing, we know how to struggle, we know how to stretch finances and meals. No one taught us to depend on the wisdom and knowledge we got from God. We learned from our experience, and we explored America. Sometimes I wonder if all the races will ever work together and love one another and put all differences aside, but it's funny to me how blacks don't look for that to happen. We talk about going over yonder, we look for the other side because we feel it's not going to happen here. We as blacks today are in heaven on earth compared to what things were like in history. We enjoy central air, going to grocery stores, living, and traveling without being off limits and without reading 'no blacks allowed'. I just don't want us to forget where we came from or take it for granted because there was a lot of hurt to get us to where we are today. We should all shed a tear for those that had no shoes, no clothes, outhouses, endured the cold winters with no central heat, little to no food, no refrigerator, no hygiene products, and holes in their roofs. We need to know our history. We need to see pictures, read stories, and see how blessed we really are now. Tears carry so much burden, and there is a story in every teardrop. Blacks should be authors because they have so many stories to tell from our hearts and minds.

We should be some of the greatest songwriters and be honored in society today because we have lived and watched God bring us a mighty long way. Some may wonder how we can still be here standing. It is nothing, but by the grace of God. No other race has stood the test like the blacks, and we still smile even though we have been wounded. This book is not written because I am a racist. It is written based on facts, opinions, and experience; people don't have to like us, but we must love each other. I have some family members I love, but I don't fool with them. If they need me, I'll come running. People don't have to love me, but respect me and I will respect them, know your history. Don't just read one book, read two or three and comprehend what you read. Then dissect it, pass it on and encourage people to go get that book and read it. There are plenty of libraries and information is readily online.

AN HONORABLE BLACK LEADER NAMED MLK

One of the finest black men in my eyes is Martin Luther King, Jr. (MLK). I am guilty of not participating in the celebration of his birthday. The first celebration I can talk about was in 1989 or 1990 in Fort Worth Texas. The parade lasted for thirty minutes. There were approximately thirty horses, ten trucks, a couple cheerleaders and a few politicians on floats. I saw one high school band and said to myself, "That's a man that had done so much and yet there is so little recognition." Then again, I had to look at myself. What was my contribution, what sacrifice had I made to honor his legacy. It was at that moment that I realized I had to stop complaining about what others weren't doing and contribute. I realized I might be the one to bring about a change if I at least did my part. We are quick to talk, but slow to move. I learned that some black people look for faults instead of helping to find solutions. MLK was a man of change, love, and passion for his black people. He listened to what people had to say, went to places he wasn't welcomed, and even when he was threatened, he didn't let that stop the movement. He said things Caucasian people didn't want to hear but he didn't waver because he was speaking the truth. Sometimes, the truth comes with a price; sometimes death is the price and he put his life on the line. I know of no other man than Jesus Christ that was willing to sacrifice his life for others. I truly believe that MLK was sent by God; he never came with violence, he came with humility and respect. He was not perfect, but he gave everything he could for others to have equal rights and justice for all mankind.

MY HISTORY OF RACISM

MY EYES HAVE SEEN

IT BASICALLY STARTED when I was five years old. I was with my grandmother at the grocery store in Pine Bluff, Arkansas on Second Street, next to an older, Caucasians only club called Yesterdays. About fifteen years later a black man named Melvin Monroe eventually came to Pine Bluff, Arkansas from Ohio, reopened the same club and called it Fat Daddy's. Grandmother and I would enter the store, and she would place me in a buggy and proceed to the produce department, where the Caucasian guy that owned the store would make his presence known. I always looked for him to come out whenever we went; he would wear a Caucasian shirt with a nice black tie, have his hair slicked back, and would intentionally be very nice to my grandmother. Although I was five, I could recognize that his intentions were not pure. As we proceeded to shop, he would continue to follow us around the store, making sure my grandmother had everything she needed. By the time we reached the counter, he would be waiting to check us out himself almost every time we visited the store. I remembered him saying, "You don't have to pay for your groceries." Grandmother would respond, "Yes, I am able to pay, and I've told you I am married." He would bag the groceries and proceed to push the buggy out to the car. During that time, I would hear him say things to my grandmother like "You are so pretty, you smell so good, you are not like the others, and you are different" while placing the groceries in the car. Before my grandmother passed at 85 years old in 1990, she reminded me about how Caucasian men would always approach her in different stores. I said, "Momma I remembered that Caucasian guy." She said I was too young to remember that guy, and asked what store it was. I said on Second Street, and she said yes. This was unheard of since blacks and Caucasians had very little dealings with each other. Another incident I recall involves my great grandfather in North Little Rock, Arkansas. Some Hispanic guys came by on a truck; there were 10 in the back and 2 in the front. They pulled in the yard while we were on the porch and started talking about repairing the roof. They spoke no English, but my great grandfather understood a little of what they were trying to say. I was seven or eight, so I went inside and got out of the grown folks' conversation. About 30 minutes later, I could hear loud talking around the side of the house. All ten Hispanics had surrounded my great grandfather demanding $1,500 after they supposedly did the work without his permission by spraying some type of chemical on the roof. He explained he had never been told the cost of the repair. Then, the Hispanic guy told him it would cost $1,200, to which my great grandfather explained that he didn't have that either. My great grandmother was not home. I soon came out of the house with the rifle cocked, pointed it at them and demanded they leave. They never returned. Later, we talked to other black families and found out that these Hispanics were going into black neighborhoods and intimidating older blacks in my neighborhood. After this incident was over, my great-grandfather said, "I don't ever want you to pull a gun on anyone." I replied, "I was not going to let anyone hurt my great-grandfather." He said he understood, and we never talked about it again.

In 1975, my grandmother and I were at my cousin, Lady Bell's house in North Little Rock, Arkansas, Lady Bell had a gift of being able to sew anything without using a pattern and her house was filled with material in every room. She was a very sweet person; however, I didn't like going into her house because of her mean dog, Queenie, a light brown Lab that would bite anyone on site. Lady Bell would put Queenie in the bedroom, and you could hear her trying to tear the door down to get to you. That day I decided to sit out on the porch. As I looked down to the end of the block, I noticed six Caucasian boys on their bikes playing, and I decided to walk by and see what kind of fun they were having. They were playing in an old cow trailer (cowboys and Indians), so I decided to join them. When I went into the cow trailer, they all ran out and locked me in. Originally, I thought it was part of the game until they left and never returned. For about an hour I was trying to get out, and I began to panic because I could see that it was beginning to get dark. I knew my grandmother was worried and didn't know where I was. A Caucasian guy who had brought groceries at a nearby convenience store passed by and I knocked and asked him to help me get out. He looked at me like *how did you get in here?* He then sat his groceries down on the ground and unlatched the door. I realized at that moment that all I had to do was stick my hand out and unlatch the latch myself. He then picked up his groceries and left. I ran back to the porch and my grandmother never realized I had left. I recognized I was very hurt that the boys treated me like that and that's when I started to notice real racism. Townsend Park in Pine Bluff, Arkansas, was the only place that blacks were allowed to swim. It looked like a high school football game on a Saturday or Sunday because it appears as though every black person in the city was there. You would see women with their kids having picnics all over the park, a D.J. and teacher named Self Win would play music, there would be a snow-cone man on site and over 100 kids would be in the pool at one time, leaving almost no room to swim.

Moreover, at least 30 people would be standing in line on the diving board. Townsend Park was known as a greeting ground for all the blacks in Pine Bluff, but I saw it quite differently. I felt that it was a shame that Townsend Park was the only place for blacks, as large as the city was. By the time I reached high school, the pool had been covered over in cement. I also looked at that as a slap in the face to the blacks in the community.

The Boy's Club was an all-Caucasian boys club on 9th street, in an all-black neighborhood. We would play sandlot football on Saturdays and Sundays on their old baseball field, because they were not using it anymore. I lived on 2nd street. One day in broad daylight, I had to use the bathroom, so I went up to the building and everyone said I wouldn't be allowed in. I was 11 years old and was told I couldn't enter. The lady behind the desk said I couldn't use the restroom, so I asked where I could use it. She said, "I don't know, but you can't use it in here." So, I went out into the weeds to take a pee. Cherry Street was the road that led to the hospital, and only Caucasian people lived on the street. If you needed to go to the hospital, you had to travel along this road. On Friday and Saturday nights, Caucasian people would have their shirts off drinking beer and throwing tissue up in the trees, sitting on lawns, looking like an all-Caucasian parade. Blacks avoided this street unless they had to go to hospital, otherwise it was off limits to blacks on Friday and Saturday nights. I remember as a young kid being terrified and sliding down in my seat when my grandfather had to take my grandmother to the hospital one night as we drove by. The family that ran the skating rink didn't respect blacks but wanted you to come and spend money. On Wednesdays and Sundays, it would be packed. On rainy nights, the Caucasian police officer would keep black kids standing at the door in the rain for no reason, just being ugly. The black kids would be soaked by the time they were allowed to enter the rink, and were treated even worse, once they did get in. Usually, the rain would have ended by the time we were ready to leave; however, I remember one Sunday night it continued to rain way past the time to leave. At midnight, the same Caucasian officer made us immediately clear out of the skating rink. He herded us out like cattle. People had to wait for their parents across the street in the rain, in a field of tall grass, with the lights off in the parking lot, for about twenty minutes and we had no access to the phone to call our parents to pick us up. A few weeks later, I recall walking with my Caucasian female friend past the Caucasian kids' locker area. We were at Dial Junior High School, laughing and talking with each other when suddenly, one of the Caucasian guys at the locker yelled, "nigger lover" to the Caucasian female that I was walking with after lunch. I turned and walked back to him and looked him directly in his face and asked him to repeat the comment he had just made. There he stood, refusing to open his mouth as my Caucasian friend begged me not to do anything to him. My Caucasian friend was totally embarrassed, but we remained friends until we later went on to college, where she eventually stopped speaking to me. I was hurt because we had been friends since middle school. It got to a point where I would stand in front of her on our college campus and call her name, to which she would avoid me at school. Eventually I stopped trying to be her friend. I was disappointed that she let racism get between our friendship. Now, years later, she found me on social media, and we began speaking again, even though we've not seen each other face to face.

In junior high, my friends and classmates called me O.B. I was considered a super athlete, was well dressed, and had a beautiful spirit that would attract a lot of girls. These females would often end up in competition to show me how they felt about me. In the 9th grade, during Christmas, they all wanted to buy me a gift. The Caucasian girls all met me at the Broadmoor movie theater, and they asked what I wanted. Those same five girls bought almost everything I had asked them for, from Polo shirts to Obsession cologne. However, one Caucasian girl bought something I felt was totally inappropriate, and through the years, I wondered why she bought what she did because I neither expected it from her nor understood the reason. The gift she bought was a black monkey holding a banana in his hand. Later, she explained that she thought it was cute, and it was, but everyone else felt it was inappropriate. As I got older, I understood what the monkey symbolized and why everyone felt it was offensive.

While in the 9th grade, my mother and I had some problems. As a result, she had sent me to live with my grandmother for about a week. During this time, I had a Caucasian friend whose family was wealthy, and I confided in him that I might be moving to Little Rock with my great grandmother because my great grandfather, who had raised me, had recently passed. My school and my community recognized I was a gifted football player and track runner. One evening when I got home from school, I heard my grandmother on the phone talking to my great grandmother. My great grandmother explained that someone had started coming to the back door of her house and had been twisting the doorknob since my great grandfather died. The next morning, I called a cousin and asked to use his motorcycle to drive to Little Rock to check on my great grandmother. She was shocked to see me. I went to my closet, got my rifle, sat on the porch and started cleaning the rifle. I was attempting to send a message to whoever was coming to my great grandmother's door. Then I got my grandfather's twelve-gauge shotgun and went on the porch with it, sending a strong message to whoever was coming to her back door. My great grandmother got off the phone, came on the porch and asked what I was doing there, I replied that I was just cleaning the guns like I said I would. When I returned home, I found out that my Caucasian friend had told his father, and his father told the superintendent that I might be leaving the school and moving out of town. Both came to me during the next game. His father and the superintendent both came to check on me, and my friend's father asked me to come to their house for dinner. I didn't know the dinner was specifically to talk to me. My friend had an older brother who didn't hang out with blacks. As we were sitting at the table, the dad started explaining why they invited me to dinner. "Marvin, we know the kind of athlete you are, and the team needs you," he said. He asked how things were going with my mom, and I replied, "About the same." Then he asked, "How would you feel about coming to live with us?" I began looking around at the house and his family, imagining how my life would change being a part of this family, finally having my hands on the better things in life. After a while, I responded, "I wouldn't have a problem living with you all, because for the most part, I really got along well with the family." The dad said, "Well, we really need you here in Pine Bluff leading the team." The older brother looked at me and said he wouldn't mind if I came to live with them, the mother said she wouldn't mind, and my friend and classmate happily said that he wouldn't mind. So, they asked me to think about it. We finished dinner, after which I left and went home. A couple of days passed, and my friend asked me if I had made up my mind. I began looking at everything they had and the little we (my family) had. The Lord spoke to me and said, '*If you do that, you will embarrass the family; like a slap in your family's face*.' A black child had never been raised by a Caucasian family in Pine Bluff that I know about. The more I thought about their proposition, the more I could see my mother's face and hear the hurt in her voice, in my head. Finally, I told the dad it would look bad on my family as if they didn't care about me, allowing me to go off and live with people that weren't related to me, and it would put a scar on the family, therefore, embarrassing them for me to move just to play sports. The father said, "Marvin, I understand, and I am glad you considered how your family would feel." I distinctively remember a Caucasian classmate I had in high school. We were in the seventh through twelfth grade together. He was a real cocky guy that often displayed his dislike for blacks. He did something in the seventh grade that I will never forget. I was sitting on a bench in the locker room at football practice with my head down and he backed into my face, spread his butt cheeks and farted in my face. He didn't run, he just laughed. I jumped up ready to retaliate, but one of my Caucasian players intervened, so I just warned the teammate to never disrespect me again. Three years later, I encountered him at a Oklahoma Drill during football practice, and each time I won, I watched him turn purple. I embarrassed him on three occasions that day. I made it my business to wait for him to come out after showering and I said, "Tomorrow is going to be the same way." He mumbled under his voice 'nigger', and I asked him what he had said, and he repeated it. I grabbed him by the neck and squeezed as hard as I could. The coaches stopped it, then I explained what he said; they made both of us go our separate ways. He eventually transferred, went to a much smaller school across town. I never saw him again, but I pray he has changed.

In my junior year, I was the starting linebacker for my team. We went to Germantown Tennessee to play a team that was all Caucasian, and ranked number one in the state, and undefeated. They were known to be prejudiced. There was a carnival held on campus and I was dressed, standing outside the field house. I was shocked when I heard a little Caucasian girl, aged five or six passing and said *'nigger go home'* to me. She kept repeating it, louder and louder *'nigger go home'.* I told my coach what happened, and he replied, "What did I tell you?" That night during the pep talk by the coach, he talked about early experiences with people who felt like this. He told us, "After we win this game, don't shake hands, don't come back to the dressing room, run to the bus." Just as the coach had instructed, after the game, we ran to the bus and got on. The Caucasian spectators ran out of the stadium and came rocking the bus.

Another event I believe impacted me greatly was during the 10-year class reunion in Pine Bluff Arkansas. Black and Caucasian schoolmates came together for the first time in 10 years. We had a ball, so much so that most of us were not ready for the night to come to an end. There was only one place left open at the end of the night, a place called Hot Rods. Though it was considered an all-Caucasian establishment, we figured in the spirit of class reunion, it would be okay to join our Caucasian schoolmates, so we all left together headed for Hot Rods. One of the Caucasian guys in the group said, "Let me go in first and make sure there is enough room for all of us." He returned to the cars a few minutes later and said, "I'm sorry, but the blacks would not be allowed to go inside the establishment." I have always believed my gift for barbering would be the one way that I could build relationships and find growth. After having two barber shops in Arlington Texas, I found another location of interest on Cooper Street in the same town. It was a beautiful building from the outside, and I could tell that it would be a gold mine. After several inquiries I was able to locate the owner of the building, an older Caucasian guy that lived in Sherman, Texas. We talked almost daily on the phone and had some great conversations, so much that I adopted him as an older Uncle who was in his 70s. We would talk about everything from family to life in general. The owner became so comfortable with our phone relationship that he informed me that the key for the building was next door at another business and I could feel free to get the key as needed to show family, friends, investors, whomever necessary, the inside of the building. Everyone was excited about the prospect of working at this new location. I was so excited that I couldn't sleep at night. I felt God was up to something unique in my life, and this building would prove to be an abundant blessing. I speak very fluently, careful to use proper diction and articulation and often hear that my dialect was not of an individual from Pine Bluff Arkansas. Based on what happened with this situation, I came to understand what I had been told, on an entirely different level. The day had finally come for me to meet with the owner of the building, which I had already perceived as just a formality at this point. This was surely going to be a signing of the lease and exchange of the rental for the building. However, when the guy pulled up and recognized who I was, it was as if he had seen a ghost. When he saw that I was black, the entire conversation and demeanor changed. Keep in mind, in previous conversations, he had explained that several individuals had contacted him concerning the building, but through our phone relationship, he was sure I was the person that he wanted to have the building. The owner said that he was starting to feel ill and needed about an hour to compose himself. He said that he would go and get himself something to eat and meet me back at the building in an hour. Well after an hour passed, the guy hadn't returned, so I dialed his number. There was no answer. I dialed the number at least twenty times, and because I did recognize that the guy had appeared to become very ill during the initial greeting, I began to get worried about him. Additionally, the weather that day was also a concern I had; it had been previously snowing. I continued to frantically call his number. However, neither he nor his wife answered the phone. I thought something might have happened to him, so I attempted to drive on the snow-covered roads, and almost headed to Arlington Memorial Hospital, which was close, to see if he might have ended up there. Nevertheless, I decided that if something had happened, his wife would contact me, so I figured I'd better get out of the cold myself. I returned home and once again attempted to contact the two numbers I had been previously using to contact the owner, no answer. A week went by with me trying to reason in my mind what could have happened, and I was led to use a different phone to attempt calling. Immediately his wife answered the phone. I felt like someone who had been asked on a date, sitting dressed and patiently waiting, but the date never arrived. I concluded that the couple had changed their mind about renting the building to me after they found out I was black. I didn't say anything to his wife on the other end, I just told my friend whose phone I was using, that he could hang up the phone.

In another scenario, my wife said she wanted a new Lexus GS300 Pearl Caucasian with tan leather, her favorite car, so I went to the Lexus dealership in Dallas. Mind you, this was over 20 years ago. I went to the dealership by myself, to surprise her. The car was on the showroom floor as you walked in, sitting on a ramp. The salesman greeted me as I walked in, and I asked him about that car. He said the car was selling for $36,000. "Everyone wants this car, and we only have one." I said, "Let me fill out an application and see what happens." My credit score was 720. While we waited, he said, "Let me show you our certified cars, a green one selling for $27,000 and blue one that sells for $28,000. I said, "I was inquiring about the Caucasian one." He said, "I'm trying to save you some money." When we went back into the office, I decided I wasn't going to do business with this guy. I'm looking at a brother, and we are making eye contact. When I left the dealership, I called them back and asked for the black guy and was connected.

I told him I didn't want to deal with the Caucasian guy anymore because he took me out on the patio to show me a different car. I felt that was an insult. The black guy told me he was sorry that happened. He told me to come back and deal with him. The next day I was called by the dealership and was told I was approved but needed $1,500 down. I said, "If I was approved, why $1,500?" I asked. "As good as my credit was, why do I have to put anything down?" The lady I was speaking with put me on hold. She quickly clicked back and informed me that she would be able to accept $1000. She put me on hold once again, and then said she could accept $500.00. Once again, I questioned the need for a down payment and finally she stated no down payment would be required, that I could come and sign the rest of the paperwork and pick up the car when I liked. The black guy had taken care of the deal and made sure I didn't have to put no money down, so I gave him a tip to show my appreciation. The Caucasian guy missed the deal because he assumed I needed something cheaper than what I asked for originally.

Shortly before the COVID-19 epidemic had been categorized, my mother and I were attending a relative's homegoing celebration in Pine Bluff, Arkansas. We both had COVID-19 and were not aware that we had contracted the illness. My mother wanted to stay for a while after the service to have a chance to meet and spend time with family members that she hadn't seen in a while, so we did. I learned that the owner of the hotel we were staying was from Pakistan. We had already been at the hotel for two weeks prior to my cousins' memorial services. One of my friends from Pine Bluff had worked for the owner and was able to get us a good deal on the room ($50.00) per night. Two weeks later another relative passed and we had to make a return trip. We decided to return to the same hotel. This time, the guy was out of town and his wife was in charge. She informed me of the cost of the room would be $60.00 per night. I explained to her that I had just recently stayed at the hotel before her husband left, and he had charged me $50.00 per night. She stated that it was between her husband and me and that she had nothing to do with that; she repeated that the cost of the room would be $60.00 per night. I asked her to look up my name and it should verify the discount her husband gave to me. She did and recognized I'd told her the truth. Subsequently, she extended me the same offer her husband had. I paid her the $50.00 for the first night and informed her that I would bring the $50.00 for the next night on the next day. The next morning, a friend came by the hotel to take me to breakfast, and we ended up eating and talking past noon. When I realized how late it was, I remembered my mother had not eaten and called her to ask if she would like me to bring her something from the restaurant. She stated that she had talked to one of her cousins and he was going to pass by the hotel and bring her favorite Chinese takeout. When I returned to the hotel, a cousin that I'd not seen for over ten years had already arrived with food for my mother. I sat and started reminiscing about old times and forgot about going to the office to pay the other $50.00. Suddenly, a key was opening the door of the hotel room we were in, and the owner's wife opened the door wide and stepped in asking for the money I owed her. There had been no phone call, no knock, no excuse me, she just busted in and asked for the money in a very harsh manner. I went over to my suitcase, paid her the money and attempted to explain it was an error on my part; however, she was not listening to anything I was trying to say. I waited for about ten to fifteen minutes and eased out of the room, away from my mother and cousin and went to the front desk. There was an African American lady behind the counter, and I asked her if the owner was around. She said she was upstairs in her room, and that she would call for her to come down. She came to the desk and asked how can I help you? I said to her, "I need you to understand that I am black, but I am also a human being." She asked what I meant. I said, "You just disrespected me, mother and my family. You burst into the room and demanded your money." I continued, "First, I know I was wrong for not remembering to come back and pay you, but I feel you treated me badly by just opening the door. I feel that if I was a Caucasian man in a suit and tie, you would have not done that. You didn't consider our privacy." She said she didn't come in, that she just opened the door. I explained that she startled us. She said, "I can just give you the money back and you go somewhere else." I started explaining that we didn't live in the area, and all blacks aren't the same, not all blacks are bad people. "I don't want my money back, I'm just trying to get an understanding," I continued. I asked her for a moment to put herself in my place and consider how she would have felt. Now that she had calmed down, she stated she wouldn't have felt good. She then said, "Okay, I get it." I responded we would be alright. The next day, as I prepared to check out, I went to the front to get the cart and we waved at each other as I passed her. She said, "Are we cool?" and I said, "Yes." She watched as I put the cart back, and asked if I would like a bottle of water. It was evident she felt remorseful and understood her incorrect approach to dealing with the prior situation. Fast-forward to the middle of 2020 and I'm in the BBVA bank in Bedford, Texas, now known as PNC Bank. I had come to the bank to sign some papers. I started talking to one of the bankers, an Indian guy, as the line in the bank started filling up. He asked me what I thought about then President Trump. I said, "I really don't like to talk about it because, I'm not a Trump follower." A guy standing in line interrupted the conversation and spoke, "Trump is the best President we have ever had." I said, "Says who?" He replied loudly, "He has done more than any other President we ever had!" The banker and I just looked at each other. I had on my niece's class shirt, class of 2000. The guy asked me if I had just graduated high school. He said, "I was looking at your shirt and wondering about your age." I said, "Man, I'm 53." I am waiting to set up my business account, and the guy continues to ramble on about President Trump. Eventually a black guy comes from one of the offices and calls my name. We go into his office, and he closes the door behind us. As we were taking care of business, the Caucasian guy from the line burst into the office and said, "There you are! I was looking for you. I just wanted to let you know that Trump has done a lot for this country." I wanted to tell him how disrespectful that was to just burst in talking about Trump again. The banker and I just looked at each other wondering how he could be so rude. That's what I mean by a black man or a black woman not having value or respect in the year 2020. This is still going on. How do we get respect? I am glad you asked. We must come firm and bold and put these types of people in their place and when we do that, they consider us hostile and a threat to their safety. In other words, we must speak up or we will never get the respect we deserve.

Now here I am at fifty-five years old working for Lyft in downtown Dallas on a sunny, Monday waiting on my Lyft client to come outside in front of the Westin Hotel on Main Street. It was about eleven o'clock in the morning. I had picked up this Caucasian client earlier, he had been in town for a conference all weekend. Midway on our way to the airport, he realized he couldn't find his wedding band which he stated he had never taken off in ten years except for this weekend since he was having an affair while he was here in town. Me, being married, I could only imagine, how he was feeling because he could not go back to Pennsylvania without the wedding band. He said the band was either in the suitcase or in the hotel room. So, I pulled over and allowed him to spend about ten minutes going through the suitcase and all his pockets and found no ring. So, I told him, "I will take you back to the hotel". He was so surprised, and asked, "Are you sure?" I said, "Sir, I can't imagine you going back home with that ring, it's there, look under the covers, under the bed, in the bathroom or on the floor. It's there I believe it". So now I am here on Main Street waiting for him to return and an elderly Caucasian man, about 80 years old with a Dallas Cowboy cap on his head walked in front of my car. I thought he was just crossing the street, but to my shock, he turned, hocked and spit on the hood of my car. I didn't know what to do and mind you I just had gotten my car washed earlier that morning. The only thing I think of in that moment was to roll down the window and ask, "Are you alright?" He walked up to my window and told me, "I am parked in the wrong place, and I need to move my damn car". Before I knew anything I jumped out of my car and ran up to him, ready to crush him. I got in his face and started to holler and curse him at the top of my lungs. Our encounter was so loud that it seemed as if I could hear my own voice echoing all over downtown Dallas. When I turned around, I saw about fifty cars at the red light, with their windows down and their cameras up recording and this man was trembling so badly in fear to the point that he had stopped talking and because he also realized the power and the size I had. In that moment God spoke to me and told me that this guy has a mental problem along with racism and I felt bad for him as well as remembering I had a grandfather. How would I have felt if someone had beat up my grandfather at this age. I also knew all those people who were filming would show me attacking this old man without knowing the full reason why this was taking place. I then got back in my car so that I could further calm down and the old man came back to window and told me to move my car across the street because this is where the bus picks me up. I gave him a look letting him know that you have been warned and told him, "Sir I am waiting for my client" and he said," Well wait for him across the street". About that time my client came out all excited and said, "I found it you were right!" All I could do was sit there and tell him, "Give me a minute, I just had a run in with this old man". My client wanted to press me for the details, but realized I was in no condition to discuss the events. When I could finally gain my composure, I drove away and as I looked back in my rearview mirror, there were several cars parked along that same street. There was nowhere for a bus to park any way. So, I thank God that I didn't do anything stupid just because he did something stupid and for my upbringing.

My brothers and sisters, this is not your average everyday book read. This book details the experience I have lived, watched, listened to and learned from after fifty-five years of observation. People are hurting all over the world. I thought it was just blacks, but I have realized that Caucasian people, Hispanics and others are hurting as well; I even thought that all rich people were happy, but I found out that most are also hurting, so what does this mean? You never know what a person is going through; just because they have money, a big house, drive a nice car and their kids go to private schools doesn't mean they are happy. When I ride through some of the rich neighborhoods like Highland Park, Frisco and some parts of Fort Worth, I say to myself, *'What did they do to get this? Who did they step on? Was the education they received from TCU or SMU?'* When I try to answer my own questions, from my observation, there are those whose success comes from the labor and the backs of black ancestors, labor sweat, blood, and tears of black ancestors. One of my biggest prayers and I cannot stress it enough is that black people will one day wake up. It's almost like we are dreaming and snoring on Grandmother's couch with the covers over our head. I wish all man and women could wake up, stop passing by each other as strangers and just stop to speak and ask: "How are you doing, Sir?" Pay compliments. I wish that our women could grow up to be respectable women for themselves and others. If there is anything a young girl is paying attention to, it is their mother and grandmothers and what examples are shown. If there is anything a little boy is looking at, he is looking for a father figure. So, I'm sorry to say in most cases, there is not one, so who do we look to? Can you answer the question? When I see women and grandmothers the ages of thirty to forty years old having tattoos all over their bodies, fake hair running down their backs, some have tattoos on their faces and necks, that cover their arms, necks and hands, Young Black Queens, God has made you beautiful, "Why would you destroy your bodies?" Most black women's mouths are so foul with filth and when you listen to the words that flow from their mouths, you wonder who their parents or grandparents are. One of the big questions is, "Where did we go wrong and how can this be fixed?" We must get back to respecting one another and ourselves. As young people, we are going to make more than one mistake. The excuses may range from "I didn't have a father, my mother was on drugs", but sometimes you must look around and see what others are doing. How did he or she become successful? Maybe you should ask her, maybe you should hang around them and listen to what they have to say about success instead of being mad and hateful, because I feel that God has provided all of us the tools necessary to thrive and be productive. Back in the day, we used to call it jealousy. Today, it is called hating and it still the same thing. It's okay to ask for help; that's not embarrassing, what is embarrassing is that you didn't ask for help, and it was all around you in this world. This world is designed for you to fail. What I mean is, if they told you the secrets or ingredients, no one would buy the cake. If they move you up the ladder, up to positions in the company, would you want to own the company? It is designed for you to be a renter not an owner, for you to buy not sell, it is designed for you to be sick and need pharmaceuticals, it is designed for you to stay in churches so that you can also stay humble. Don't get me wrong I love the church and thank God we were given religion, because in this corrupt world, the church keeps us humble. Can you imagine blacks with no church? Some may say the Bible is not true, that is their choice; I believe in the Bible. It has kept me humble, kept me focused and kept me reaching for a higher understanding of '*What He does for others, He can do for me.*' The church gives me hope as my uncle Wealthy O'Bryant would say. It is what it is. Can you imagine when blacks had nothing, we loved, cared, looked out for each other, watched and fed others' kids. What a community that was. When I was a little boy, I didn't see all the rude children disrespecting their mothers and fathers. Siblings might argue, fuss and push, but they didn't fight each other because they knew that when their father got home, he didn't care who had started the fight...he would be the one to finish it. The ladies that you would pass on the way home standing on the porch and knew about what you had done, would stop you and whip you, your grandparents might be home when you got there and that would get you another whipping before your mother and father got there. Those whippings worked to keep us in line but look what has happened now? I agree that we should not abuse our children, but discipline is needed. I have heard of some blacks not whipping their children to instill discipline and they turned out alright, but, some of us needed those whippings to stay in line, and I thank God for mine, some may have needed a few more. The reality of how blacks raised their children in the past based on what we see happening now is one of the reasons I woke up black. I recognized that all those years and tears that it took for the village to raise me, had finally paid off. I was able to hold my head up and be counted as a strong, independent and intelligent black man that had overcome the challenges and obstacles previously mentioned in this book. Today, my wish is that you see those coming behind me that desire to be counted as equal also.

Growing up, I always felt embarrassed and worried about what people thought of me or what I was wearing. I felt that the proper clothes made a big difference. I must say I have learned a lot about the Caucasian men and women, and some have been good things. Being young, I used to watch them closely. I wondered about so many things that I saw differently about them, how they were able to dress so nicely, if learning was as hard for them, why they had braces, and I didn't? I watched them remember to grab their lunch boxes before we went into the cafeteria, because they never ate the school lunch, and it was impressive seeing them stand in front of the class with their homework completed. One of the greatest things I observed they did was to stick together, and I was amazed at how different things worked in their world. If there is one thing that I would like to encourage blacks to do, is to stop complaining so much, start learning ways that we can survive like they do, and even how they come together to get things done in the business world. They are no different from us; they just choose to operate with a different mindset. I hope not to offend anyone, because they have been taught the game and we are still trying to figure it out. One of the games is entrepreneurship, being in control, having property to sell. Buying land starts with going to school, getting an education so that you can make a future for you and your family and build generational wealth. I must truly say sometimes it hurts to go home and ride through the neighborhoods and see where I lived. My plans are to find ways to bring resources to my old communities and share knowledge with those that are coming behind me. I would hope that others would engage my vision for the community and share their knowledge and resources to keep the community from going down. They need the knowledge of having their own business and owning their own houses. Let them know that they don't have to make giant steps, but they must do something.

I grew up under the pressure of being the youngest of three siblings and the last to leave home. It was no different from the pressure of unscrewing the top of a coke bottle too fast. Sometimes the pressure will cause it to explode, but I found out I was not alone. No one is teaching black kids about finding themselves, their gifts and talents; everyone is saying 'go to school get your education'. But what is it for, if you don't know what you want to do, or what you want to be? No one is helping each other in black families; we don't tell our children the truth. They are left to figure things out for themselves. I would like to tell young black children this: "If you have eyes to see and ears to hear you are never too young to learn." I hate to hear people say that they are too young to do this or that. They need to hear what the Bible says: it says to train up a child in the way they should go, and when they're old they will not depart from it; it also says if you spare the rod, you ruin the child, so if that is what the Bible says, then parents should follow what it says. I once heard my uncle Charles O'Bryant say, "You have to teach a child that 'no' means 'no', 'yes' means 'yes' and 'maybe' means 'we might, or we might not'. 'Go sit down means go sit down;' if you say 'stop', you don't let them keep going, because if you don't stop as a child, you might not like the outcome. Discipline hurts, and sometimes you may cry as the parent. Who wants to see their child in a room while everyone else is playing? However, you must punish them if they disobey. You must let them learn to think before they react. One of the worst things I have seen is a grown person making child-like mistakes. If you don't believe me, look in the penitentiary; the women and men are not young. So where did we go wrong as black people, we stopped showing love for each other, we stopped respecting ourselves and each other, we don't spend time talking to each other, we don't love each other like we used to, we don't complement each other no more. What happened? It appears that the plan to separate us is really working. All I'm saying is *Black people wake up*.

I used to wonder why growing up at eleven years old, you would hear people say that when you are eighteen, you must get a job and leave my house. I wondered why eighteen would always be the magic number they said, and then after having a conversation with my grandparents and my mom, I realized it was because at eighteen, you were considered 'grown'. The flip side of that is hearing "Since you're eighteen, you will want to run my house, change my rules. You should start to make your own choices and decisions." This is called responsibility. We shouldn't wait until we are twenty-six to start having responsibility, it starts early even childhood.

HATRED-PREJUDICE

I'm afraid of anyone that says they hate someone. I can't even be around someone that says they hate someone. That word hatred is foreign to me because I wasn't raised like that. I am against hate. How do you hate someone for being who they are? It's okay to dislike or not fool around with people but I can't even understand not speaking to someone to show you hate them in 2023. I'm afraid for them because it takes serious energy to hate. Their facial expression makes them look like monsters because it takes so many muscles to frown. Can you imagine the energy it takes for you to hold your mouth to say I hate him or her? The only thing I do is pray for this person and pray they don't hurt the other person physically, emotionally, or verbally. Hatred is dangerous.

WHAT DO WHITE PEOPLE THINK ABOUT BLACK PEOPLE?

Most Caucasian people will say, "I like black people". I can't really answer for a Caucasian person. I can only go by what I have heard some say. I will say *show me instead of telling me*. I'm not judging, but to me I think that other blacks will agree. Being from a small city called Pine Bluff, I went to the second biggest high school in Arkansas, and I can say some of us, both black and Caucasian, got along well with no fights. At school we had separate parking lots and we ignored it. As I have gotten older, I wondered why was that when we were an integrated school sharing classrooms, lockers, and football fields. We played sports together, but it was sometimes uncomfortable because I saw my black athletes walk home late at night after games, while my Caucasian teammates got in their cars and drove past us. I would never have let my Caucasian brothers walk home in the dark and I had a car. I would have picked them up even if we had to pile in the car on top of each other just to make sure everyone got home safely because if we are brothers on the field, we must be brothers off the field.

When I go to funerals, I don't see Caucasians and we don't go to theirs. We are still carrying these ways, but we see each other in a mall or in the supermarkets and hug, but from what I have seen in my immediate society, we don't support each other. We must show change rather than talk if we care, because if we want to change it's not what we say it's what we do. It's the little things that make a difference, but it starts with forgiveness.

WHAT DO BLACK PEOPLE THINK ABOUT WHITE PEOPLE?

Because I am black, I think about stories I heard, situations I saw and just living from day to day. Let me start with those that don't look like us. I think they were wrong, low down dirty. I don't believe they cared with no good intentions from the start. Using people for their advantage and once the assignment was complete, like an empty chip bag, we were thrown in the trash. Read about these stories. The problem I have is the teachings that we are getting about what happened during those four hundred years of slavery, very little has changed. We are still disrespected and treated with no value. If you look closely, Caucasians rarely speak first when it comes to greeting. In this regard, I have made up my mind, I'm not speaking first. I intentionally look to see if anyone will hold the door at a grocery store, it really doesn't happen much where I'm from. I lived across from people for five to six years and they never spoke. In this year and time, we still act like this. At this age I don't know what to think about change or sometimes the lack thereof.

THE WAY I FEEL AROUND WHITE PEOPLE

There is not a day that I don't feel fear because I know you don't value who I am, so I have to prove myself worthy. I'm fifty-five years old, and I still feel that way. The entire time I'm with a Caucasian person, I'm trying to convince them that I'm not a nigger, I'm human, and I'm always on the defense, waiting for another one of them to get out of line. and that's sad. I get a question asked quite frequently: will things ever change? Growing up, I was taught not to ever say "never," but I'll say "never." I've learned how to forgive, but I don't forget. There has been too much bloodshed, too much humiliation, and too many people stepped on. I tell people every day that the oldest virus in the world is racism. Some of the main things that have hurt the black community are lack of knowledge, drugs, alcohol, racial profiling, an unfair jury of your peers, laws made to keep us locked up, and living in underserved communities. To say that Black Lives Matter is an under- statement. For over four hundred years, we were stolen from our families, countries, and everything we knew and loved to build this land, and we have never been treated like anything but machines. Black people are tired.

THE WAY I FEEL AROUND BLACK PEOPLE

Where are we going as black people? We walk around without a clue, without a guide, without a vision, purpose and no unity. Where are we going? It appears to me that we are on a downhill spiral. There is no focus, no drive, no hope. That's what I see. No one is leading, no one is following, but everyone is doing some moving and talking with no plan. Where is the destination? Sitting on a dock waiting. Babies are being born, they are listening, watching and growing, depending on us as parents to make a life for them. We don't have time to wiggle our thumbs. We used to be a proud nation; even though we were hurt, and abused, we were still proud to be black. James Brown said it best in his lyrics; *say it loud, I'm black and I'm proud.* Though I can't sing it anymore, I used to sing it with joy, hope, vigor, and my chest stuck out. There was something about the way he said it. It was like he was giving you directions exactly the way it should be said. It was the way he told you to say it. He didn't tell you to whisper, he said *make it sound special, say it at the top of your voice.* "I'm Black and Proud." Proud of what? Proud to be a product of the forefathers, that contributed so much to this country. Proud that we can have museums, finally being recognized, history being unfolded, our value being shown, we can be a man, we can raise a family. The proudness for me to be in this brown skin is that I'm proud that those before us didn't give up, they had a plan and a vision. Every time they were knocked down, they got back up. They didn't break; sometimes they had to bite their lips, but they still had hope for tomorrow. You might have taken our freedom, our minds, but you didn't take our joy. Sometimes the joy has been beaten down, making us feel that there is no reason to live. I've seen a lady visit her father in a nursing home, in a wheelchair, maybe hadn't said anything all week, but the joy of finally seeing his daughter brought him so much joy, it would make him bob his head. It may have seemed that the father had no life left, because of being beat down by the distress of not having the right healthcare coverage, the distress of health, the distress of his past jobs. Times like these when you still can get up enough strength to at least bob your head for some reason, puts me in the mind of two great singers: Fats Domino and Jackie Wilson. The stimulation of seeing something that even though you may have had a rough life, gives you hope and makes you want to get up, or sit and move in your wheelchair, snap your fingers, or do a little head bounce. Where are our black leaders? We need real leadership with a firm drive in the mindset black people. We are stuck in the mud and Caucasians are looking, saying "I told you so, walking around with their pants sagging, looking like criminals. They won't get their beard washed and trimmed, won't put on decent clothing, won't brush their teeth and are comfortable with their appearance." There is nothing wrong with hip hop but put a suit on every now and then, let them see who you can be, dress up, even if there is nowhere to go, look like a leader, someone might invite you to talk. Leaders should inspire, draw others like a magnet. Those on the sidelines are standing around waiting for someone to take them by the hand and guide them, but no one is coming. We have been led for so long by people that don't really care about us, and it keeps us going to the wrong places. We are being led to the fire, to the ditches, and to poverty. We shouldn't have to wait to get to heaven to enjoy some of the things that others do; we are the ones that do all the work, why can't we enjoy some of the pleasure? We shouldn't be so quick to run to the Caucasian malls, Caucasian barbers, Caucasian grocers and even now, Caucasian churches. Every so often today, the only people we see that can enjoy their lives and not live from paycheck to paycheck are the Caucasian people, so we try to do what they do, so that we can have some of what they have, but I don't think we ever will. So many other races have joined in on making the black race look bad. This is not a racial statement, just a truthful one. From what I have seen, even many Mexicans have no respect for blacks, they are moving to the US and the government gives them benefits that we as born American citizens aren't able to get. They move here as poor people and can come here and buy a house, while we as blacks continue to struggle to just pay the rent. We must put our money in the Caucasian banks because it's so hard for a black man to own a bank and we are taught not to help each other and work together to have our own banks. The interest rates are so high at the Caucasian banks and credit issues are so tight that we can't borrow anything from them to try to get ahead. Yet, we still try to live in their neighborhoods. If you are lucky enough to move into their neighborhoods, most of the time, they won't even speak to you. They will give you so much hell, constantly calling the police on you just because, and you end up with so many violations and have so much stress, eventually you move. I have learned that even when you drive a nice car and your children go to school with their kids, they still don't really respect you. They play a good game sometimes, but black folks know what it means to hear and see sincerity. Are there anymore black leaders that won't surrender to what the Caucasian people have in place and in mind for the continued distribution of the black race? If we start sticking together, we will become much more powerful. That's why we are constantly being taught to hate, kill, and destroy each other. We need a great black leader to keep us focused on how to make things better for our race. Election time will come, and we hear about all the things that a new black elect is going to do to make things at least equal for us. He tells us to believe in him and vote for him and then he gets downtown and gets so caught up in the benefits he receives, that he forgets about us. He gets caught up in feeling like the Caucasians now accept him and allow himself to be bribed. He forgets all the hell they gave him as he tried to get where he is now. For the last thirty years of my life, I haven't seen anyone standing up and doing the right thing by blacks. We get crumbs to shut us up and keep us from complaining, organizing and demanding our fair share. Is it that fear steps in once they have a position to use it, because he is afraid to go back where he came from? Then what our ancestors fought for, and how they fought for it is disgraced by that fear. There needs to be someone to have a real voice for our communities, not disgrace the legacy of our ancestors. When an elected leader feels he or she is no longer able to be true to who he or she is, step down. We would respect them more. We are being left here as the black society to fend for ourselves. The politicians come around regularly while they are campaigning, but as soon as the person is elected, you never see them again until it's time for re-election. We know that once they are in office, they must work, but what work are they doing, because nothing is changing in our communities. If they don't come and talk to us, how will they know what we need? Or is it that they really don't care? We used to be a people that spent time getting to know each other. Neighbors knew their neighbors, the pastor knew his people in the church, the business in the community knew the people in their communities and politicians even knew some of the people in the districts they represented, but no one takes the time to get to know each other anymore. People are known now by their presence on social media or their background checks. Politicians beware. The new generation is taking more interest in their elected officials. They do not have the pastor or take the advice from their family and friends on who to vote for; they are taking the time to fact check and get to know the values of the people they are electing. They will hold the politicians to a standard.

TIRED AND DISGUSTED

Black people got tired of being walked on, spit on and beat on. I think our history needs to be taught more so that everyone knows the truth. You should look at the ones that did us like that and say *how can you be so cruel, that was evil.* Back in those days, we were hung for things like stealing chickens or merely by looking someone in the eye, and when were hung some Caucasians would bring their children along so that they would know how this was supposed to go. No doubt, I can imagine Caucasian boys standing crying, while some black man was hanging from a tree being beaten, hands tied, legs tied and having private parts cut off. It had to be disturbing to a child and adults.

Again, my question is, how can history be taken out of schools? If we are allowed to see it, let us read it and have the option to see what was right and wrong for ourselves. When a Caucasian woman marries a black man, they are happily married because they choose to love each other for who they are, and not because of their skin color. The color of their skin doesn't matter. Let's be honest, when a Caucasian woman is young, she is curious about a black man and vice versa. Blacks are curious about Caucasians. Half won't tell the truth, but Caucasian women have gone to their grave without admitting they have slept with black men and the same for Caucasian men and the results are light skinned, fair skinned children. 30% of the race is bi-racial and it's been going on since slavery. Why is that not in history books? Blacks were raped during the slavery period as if it was nothing. Caucasians didn't look at it as rape because they owned blacks like an animal, so they didn't care about blacks being married, and felt that what they were doing was okay. Today, the law states that when a human being is forced to have sex, it is rape, but who makes the law, who enforces the law? Typically, when some Caucasian men do something wrong to a black person, even if they think it's not right, in most cases, they stick together because they know that the same Caucasians will kill him and his family and burn their house down. My message, in general, is to learn your history for yourself. Learn dates and times and don't become bitter; just stay strong and don't let your guards down.

Caucasians complain about robbing, killings, and crime, but let's go back in time to history and look at the killing that Caucasians have done to blacks for no reason. My point is, reparations should be in effect and maybe if blacks are allowed some success, they could possibly forgive some of the wrongs that were done to them. They could start to release some of the pressure they feel they are always under. For the last few years, I have noticed this, and it bothers me. That is when I say hello or greet a Caucasian person in the store or on the street and s/he won't speak back. Then I speak louder to make s/he speak, if they don't I laugh and walk off saying, "Wow"!

OUR LIVES BUILT ON CULTURE

MY EARS HAVE HEARD

I WOULD LIKE TO SPEAK to black people about some very important topics that we all should build our lives around and that is ***Ethics for the Black Communities and our culture,*** which include:

1. God First,
2. Love Yourself,
3. Love Your Parents,
4. Respect,
5. Responsibility
6. ***and more…….***

GOD FIRST

First, I thank God that I was introduced to church as a kid. My great grandfather was on the deacon board, my great grandmother was on the mothers' board and my sister sang in the choir at Shiloh Baptist Church in Little Rock Arkansas. Growing up in our house, as early as four and five years old, church was not an option. We were in church with my great grandparents every Sunday. I thank God that the church was not boring; the choir was awesome, the deacons and senior choir were awesome. No one fell asleep. I looked forward to going to church where everyone seemed to be praising God and getting their worship on. It was there that I learned about the responsibility of offering and tithing. I will never forget; my great grandmother would make me write my name on the envelope, and I didn't understand it then, but now I know they needed to know where it came from. I really didn't like Sunday School much. It was too early, but I had to go because we went to church early. I became so tired of the Sunday School teacher asking me about the lesson. So one day I realized that my friend, Derrick, who was the same age that I was, would study his lesson every week and come to Sunday school prepared to answer all the questions. I became quite impressed with him, because I liked the response that he would get from the class and the teachers; everyone would clap for him at the end of his presentations. So I went home and started reading my bible and when the teacher asked me a question the next time, everyone was surprised because I knew the answer. The Sunday School was so proud of me and from then on, I made sure to study the lesson and prepare to answer questions. Soon, the teacher allowed me to give the Easter speech. This was a very important event for black children in the church. My great grandparents made sure that I was going to be prepared to deliver this speech looking very nice. I remember being dressed in an all-Caucasian suit with a powder blue tie, and a handkerchief that was given to me by my great grandfather. I knew I looked the part and thought that I was ready. As the time approached for me to stand in front of everyone and give my speech, I looked out at the crowd, and it suddenly became quiet. I hurriedly walked out of the building with tears in my eyes. Fear had gotten the best of me. My great grandfather told me that it was okay and that sometimes, things like this happen. I learned something else from him that day, something that I have carried with me throughout my life. He said, "Even with something as small as an Easter speech, son, you must be prepared not only on the outside, but as well on the inside to face giants." All through life, I never knew God for myself. I heard about him all the time. As I got older, I began to read His word and understand His word, and I also learned that when I was in trouble, to call on His name. If you call Him, He will answer, but you must be patient. I also learned as a young man that no didn't always mean never, and that sometimes with God, no just meant not right now. So, once I got into a few jams that I couldn't get out of, I knew it was God that freed me from the situation. Then I started to talk to him daily, started telling him 'Thank you', 'I love you' more often and started asking what I should do. There were times I was ashamed to let my friends know how I felt about God. I would hide it… so at fifty-five, now I'm not ashamed to let you know I trust, depend and lean on God. I know for sure I made it this far by His grace; I know that I have favor, because some nights I went to bed wondering if I would wake up, and once my eyes opened, I said "Thank you Lord." Now I try to be a light to someone else with wisdom and knowledge. I don't have the money that I would like to have yet, but I have the peace of knowing that with God all things are possible in my life. Whatever you do, put God first; we can make better life decisions about situations that may happen to us or around us. When things like cheating, violence, lying, stealing, even murder, might come in our path, if we put Him first, we will come out better. One thing I want people to know is that God will give you second chances. "Just because you made a bad turn doesn't mean He won't put you on the right road. You got to let Him know that you want to do better, to change your mindset. When everyone else has walked away, He is always there to talk to, and He will answer. He promises that He will never leave you nor forsake you.

LOVE YOURSELF

I have witnessed so many people loving others and not realize they don't love themselves, going out of their way to love others, spend their last, give something they have to a person and the person not love them in return. I believe everyone, regardless of color of skin, or where we were raised, everyone needs to love himself or herself. You might feel ugly, chubby or skinny, it doesn't matter; love yourself. Some people may laugh at you or look at you sideways, but when they see the confidence, you have in loving yourself, they will leave you alone. Look in the mirror at yourself and remember that God made everything the way he wanted, and he made you just perfect. I just believe that as we go through life and as we get older, we should be able to make better decisions. There will be times in your life that the situation may look bad, but you have to say to yourself that this is not the end. Motivate yourself, even if it's just with a song that you remember from church. I have realized that this works for me. Learn how to separate yourself from others and have some time for yourself and take time to talk to God. Go shopping, buy a new car, a house, get your nails done, do something that makes you feel better about yourself and your current situation. God made others, but He made you too. He only made one of you and you should strive to be the best version of you.

LOVE AND RESPECT

It used to be difficult for me because not everyone respected and cared for me. As I grew older, I had to come to terms with this, but once I did, it became a simple matter. My grandmother had me read the scripture that talked about Jesus being crucified. Right before he passed, he asked His father to forgive them because they knew not what they were doing. I used to believe they knew, but then when I got older, I realized they didn't. I realized they couldn't be in their right mind. I thought about it like a sick child killing their parents; who in their right mind would do that? So now, when I am mistreated, I still get a little angry, but then I come around. When people call me out of my name at fifty (50), I say, "No, they don't know." The language younger people use to talk about older people breaks my heart. They live their lives being disrespectful. Some of them don't consider that when talking to their elders and each other, they should avoid using certain language. Calling older men, "Homie" and/or "Old School", are some of the examples. I have been referred to by both slangs, and I don't believe that it is appropriate. I was taught to say, "Yes Sir", "No Sir", "Yes Ma'am, No ma'am", when you are speaking to elderly people. Moreover, Caucasians can be so disrespectful to those that don't look like them, sometimes. They will be disrespectful enough to call you, "Boy" or "Gal. When you learn how to love people regardless of what they look like, you won't disrespect them.

RESPONSIBILITY

Responsibility plays such an important role in a young person's life because that's the beginning of life, to be responsible for yourself. You must pay your rent, pay your own car note, take care of yourself, eat right, go to the doctor, take care of your health, and even go to the barber and beauty shop. When it comes to your job and getting promotions, often, the person in charge won't say anything; however, they pay attention to how responsible you are by the things you do. If you are late frequently, that is not a good sign of responsibility. If you are not dressed appropriately, that plays a big part in your consideration for a promotion. Sometimes our minds are focused on so many other things while we are at work that we can't remember what we should be doing from one minute to the next and forget things that we are told to do. These are not good signs of responsibility. You must practice responsibility. In other words, people should not have to wonder if you are responsible; it should be your way of life and it should stay with you until the end of life. Back in the olden days, people's names would ring in the city if people knew that you were responsible; they knew they could depend on you. I used to hear people say, "Get Mr. Green or get Mr.

Johnson and pay him to do the job because I know he is responsible." These people were called authoritative figures because they knew a little bit about how to get a whole lot of things done, or men of wisdom or experience.

APPEARANCE

When I was in junior high school, I was being raised by a single parent. The money was never great, but we made it. Buying expensive clothing was never an option, we couldn't afford it. My mother worked hard to keep the bills paid and most of the time, there were no extras. I had a friend, an older gentleman, Roger Pleasant, that saw something in me. He could see that I wanted to be somebody and do something with my life. He told me about the thrift store. He said that I could get nice suits, Caucasian shirts, and ties and put them in the cleaners. So, I went and bought two to three suits and got them tailored. This changed my life and my appearance. In a short time, I had a large enough collection to wear suits to school every day. My barber, Ezell Pruitt at BNS Barbershop would keep my hair sharp and my grandaddy made me keep my shoes shined. My schoolmates noticed that my whole attitude had changed. The one thing that I noticed was that people treat you differently according to your appearance. They tend to respect you more. My teachers complimented me on how I looked, those same teachers began to tell certain young ladies that I should be the kind of person they should pursue for dating. I was on my way, wearing nice shirts and suits and I even started wearing cologne. Women love to smell cologne and I loved what they would say about the way I smelled. Then one day I asked my granddaddy if I could wear his watch. He responded by asking why I wanted to wear the watch. I told him that I know look nice, my shoes shined, I smell good, but I needed the watch to complete my look. Even today the watch is still a distinct accessory and a conversation piece despite the fact just about everyone has a cell phone with the time on it. He bought me my first watch that year for Christmas. These were some of the events that helped me to understand that you don't have to look like your circumstance. I started to get a lot of respect from the Caucasian community as well. They were trying to figure out who I was and if I was rich. I loved the reactions that I would get from them, the stares that I would get from them as they passed me and how different they would treat me from the other blacks in the community. As time would pass, I would learn that you must be careful when you start feeling this way about yourself, but I continued to smile like never before.

EDUCATION

Education never meant much to me growing up. I never took time for it or cared about it until the 10th grade. My counselor informed me that I had a chance to get into a division one school. So, I decided to apply myself to get into the school. Reading is what I became the most interested in. I practiced like crazy because I didn't want to settle for another school. Math came easy because I had learned early how to count my money. My mother had a lot of books in her bedroom on her bookshelf, so I started reading my mother's books. I would select two to three books at a time and read them. It wasn't very long before I fell in love with reading. I got a dictionary to learn the words that I didn't know. I learned how to take big words, break them down and learn them. Soon I was using the new words I learned every day in my conversations. Some of my classmates would ask, "What did you say?" It became fun for me to use big words that others in my community didn't know. Some of my favorite words to use were (*sophisticated, entrepreneur, bougee, sarcastic*) just to name a few. I became fascinated with how education was important when it came to communicating effectively. Learn how to ask questions. Listening is major when it comes to education. Be the one that sits in the front of the classroom paying close attention as to see the words fall out the mouth of the person teaching. Comprehending and listening go hand in hand. You must be able to comprehend what you have read. Comprehension was another word that I didn't hear much when I was growing up. I learned never to be afraid to ask questions. While others felt that their questions were dumb, they would not ask questions, but I found out that others had opinions that better explained what I had questions about. As a result, I learned that there is no dumb question when you are trying to learn. Everyone will have their own opinion, similar but different. You must have your own level of comprehension.

ADMIRATION & PASSION

I have been a person that dreamed big all my life. I was also a people watcher; I loved figuring out their personalities, loved listening to their tone and loved watching their fashion. I admire listening to people with accents and I pay attention to the way people walk. People with elegance will especially catch my attention. I feel that I am the sum of everyone I have admired. When a man sees a pretty woman dressed up, she is easily recognized. It's also important to acknowledge when a man is well dressed and groomed. I admire preachers and first ladies when they walk in the room. Some of my favorite classes of people are actors, actresses and politicians. Imagine working your way up to be Mayor or President; similarly, imagine a regular female schoolteacher working her way up to become the principal of a school. There is nothing you can't do if you put your mind to it and emulate the action required to accomplish it. Look at Tyler Perry, T.D Jakes, Michael Jordan, Denzel Washington, Oprah Winfrey, The Obamas, James Brown, Prince, Michael Jackson, and Kamala Harris. Know your surroundings, get to know the people in your community, inspire and encourage others in your community. Never get too big that you forget where you came from. I think it's most important to think before you decide.

Find your passion early in life and stick with it. Your passion is what you would do even if you didn't get paid for doing it. My first passion was hunting. My great grandfather took me rabbit and squirrel hunting for the first time when I was in the fourth grade. I was a fourth grader with a twenty-two rifle. He would hunt fifteen to twenty rabbits a day. From that point on, I would go to the store and immediately go see the hunting books; I loved it so much that unfortunately, I sometimes would steal the books from local grocery stores. When I had the money, I would buy the books then be in class reading them, looking at the clothes and equipment. I was thrilled at figuring out how to get my next bullet. Eventually, my cousin, Ray who traveled with Ziggy Marley for thirty years and was a concert promoter, came to town and introduced me to the Ohio Players. After they came to Arkansas, I left the hunting and wanted to be in music. I had met Sugar Foot ("*Skin Tight*"), the lead singer for the Ohio Players and said to myself, *that's who I want to be*. This was the first image of a man that I wanted to be. I let my hair grow and began to imitate Sugar Foot as much as possible. I left my passion, started playing the guitar and started my own group. We were called The Ice-Cold Band. My band mates were Greg Bradley, Robert Taylor, Robert Hartnett, Jayfus Gordon, Fred Wiseman, Floyd Howard, and Morris Hayes. Morris Hayes went on to play with Prince and the Revolution for thirty years. We also had female singers: Felecia Fair (lead), April Fair (sisters) and their cousin Candice. We played in talent shows, at convention centers and anywhere we could. Picture this; I was in the seventh grade singing in nightclubs. After the group broke up, that's when I got into football. I learned it and mastered it so much that it became my new passion. I ate, talked and walked like a football player, and my plan was to one day play pro football. That became all I knew, all I lived for. I would soon learn that you can't put all your eggs in one basket. Football didn't work out for me, and then I found out that as much as I had loved all the things that I had previously done, my real passion was people. It was then that I chose barbering. It was through barbering that I learned to touch all mankind. I learned patience and how to have a positive attitude. I heard grown men talk about divorcing their wives, their daughters being pregnant, I learned to listen and make a difference. My greatest pleasure early in barbering would be when single women would come in with their sons' needing haircuts. Sometimes the expressions on their face as they went into their purse to pay, would let me know they were struggling, and this haircut might mean less food at the table for dinner tonight. I would say, "You're good, that one is on me." So that's how I learned to make a difference in the lives of others, and that's why I'm writing this book today, because of my love for people. My joy is when I make a difference in someone's day. Kind words that I say to people and that they might say to me. Complimenting them on their clothes, hair, appearance and sometimes being able to give them a dollar or two, when someone walks and /or drives by throwing up the peace sign. I would hear my uncles and grandpa tell people to *hang in there, hold on, it will be alright after a while*. Now I find myself doing the same thing, telling them to hold their head up, be strong and when I get a smile from someone that I am encouraging, it brings me joy. What is your passion?

SURROUNDINGS

Everyone that's in your circle ain't in your square. Everyone that's standing behind you, don't have your back. If the room that you walk in doesn't light up, you're in the wrong room. Just because you are family by blood doesn't mean you are family by love. Blood folks can be your worst enemies. They come filled with envy and jealousy, appearing to support you, and all the time their only motive is to see what they can get from you, how they can tear you down or belittle you. I would like to tell you to surround yourself with positive, open-minded people that can motivate you to pursue your dreams. I loved to sit on the front porch of the elderly people in my community when I was younger. They would tell me stories, both good and bad, about what they had done in their lives to make it to where they were, and I began to pattern myself like them based upon the knowledge I had gained I didn't play with kids my age, because I needed wisdom and knowledge that these older, successful people had. On Sundays, we went to Greater Shiloh Baptist Church on Broadway in North Little Rock, Arkansas. There were many black churches in the community, but Greater Shiloh was like a small Potters House. Most often on Sundays and anytime the church doors were opened, there was not a seat in the house. The church would be packed, and cars would be coming from everywhere. We would drop my grandmother and sister at the door and Papa and me had to park and walk a distance to get back to the church. There were thirty to forty people in the choir, and I would see twenty to thirty families arriving in anticipation of what the Pastor had in store. Rev. Bunton was my favorite pastor, and he was from Buffalo, New York. He had five boys with big afros looking like they were a part of the Jackson 5. Pastor Bunton would get so caught up in the Word he would lean back and scream and put his hands in his pocket, looking like he was the man. We had two of the finest musicians on the organ and piano, Bobby and Gary. Bobby had processed hair and Gary had a big round afro. I admired them so much. You can grow up for years with an individual and not know their limitations and/or capabilities. Knowing our surroundings is so important and there's a song that I like by a Caucasian band, The Cars, that embodies this. The song says 'Who's gonna tell you things aren't so great, can't go long thinking nothing is wrong'.

DON'T JUDGE

What God has for others, it might not be for you and what He has for you might not be for others. In this life, the people around you may take off before you accomplish things, before you get married, get your first degree, first job, first house, first everything. You might hear some of your black friends, neighbors, relatives, schoolmates say, "How did they get that before I did?" We go judging and trying to find an answer to how they accomplished what the other person hadn't accomplished. I call that being out of your league. God blesses us in His own time, and His way so you must realize the same thing he did for them, he can do for you, but don't question God's work when you feel left behind. Keep reminding yourself that God has something for you as well.

REMEMBER WHERE YOU COME FROM

I HAD THE PRIVILEGE and the blessing of being raised by my great grandparents, John and Lucy Shelton. The neighborhood that I was raised in was called Dark Hollow, because there were no streetlights on that side of town, in North Little Rock, 811 East 16th street. My phone number at the time was 501.372.1950. I heard this phone number and address so much that I will take it to my grave because there are so many memories on that small property. There were so many bittersweet conversations that came through that phone line, so many that you can't remember them all. The mustard yellow colored phone cord stretched from the living room to the kitchen. We didn't have any phones in the bedrooms, so when it was time to go to bed, you went to bed. After supper, we watched the news, took baths, put on our pajamas, said our prayers, and went to bed. My great grandfather would stay up and watch the 10 o'clock news, while sister, my great grandmother and I would tuck down under the covers. My great grandmother would wake us at 5:30 in the morning with bacon, scrambled eggs, biscuits, onions, bell peppers and home fries before it was time for chores. As an outdoors person, I would cut the yard and my sister would fold sheets and quilts. On that property we had corn, green beans, black eyed peas, tomatoes, onions, squash, carrots, a full garden with everything you could think of, along with an apple tree, fig tree, persimmon tree and a lemon tree that came from my cousin, Louis Gaines from California. The tree produced two yellow lemons in its lifetime. Our back fence had honeysuckle growing on them (a favorite of mine), but you had to watch out for bees. Whenever my great grandmother would walk down the street, people would say 'Hello Ms. Shelton, good evening Ms. Shelton. 'Everyone knew her. My great grandfather only left the house to pay bills. After completing my chores, I would ride down the same street that my great grandmother had went previously, stopping here and there for a visit. I considered these people my friends. I am telling you this story because I am a storyteller and this is where many of the stories that I tell came from, hours spent listening to these people on their porches. So many of the lessons that I learned from the people and their stories were about how to love and to have patience. How to give respect, and dignity, how to be polite, how to smile and compliment others. Even though we were possibly considered a poor family, in my eyes, we were rich. My great grandfather built a two-bedroom house when he left the military and drove a 1964 green-on-green Buick Electra 225, but for some reason, the black community would call it a deuce and a quarter. Those were the days when a lot of blacks didn't have nice cars. I would see people staring at us when we would go out, because they thought we were rich. We would go to the grocery store; Wynne Gardens and my great grandmother would dress nice with her hair pinned up. Great Grandad would throw on a suit coat, nice shoes, and Dobb hat; we had to dress nicely, and this would happen weekly. We knew we could not go into the public looking any kind of way and that still stands with me today. I teach my children that it is important that when people meet them, especially for the first time, appearance is important. Even though I was raised in a Christian home, and we were not taught prejudice or racism of any kind, I was afraid of Caucasian people. When I would see them, I would not look them in the face, because I was so afraid of the things I had heard, seen and experienced regarding the way they treated blacks. I was afraid for my great grandparents of what might happen to them when they went to corporate buildings to pay bills. There were two big stores in the community that I remember. Mr. Bill and Mr. Pickett were Caucasian men, I must admit that they were nice men. Mr. Bill managed one store and Mr. Pickett the other. As I go through that town now at fifty-five years old, I hesitate to ride through my neighborhood and look at those old houses and reminisce on those conversations that were had in Dark Hollow. I think about some of the houses and people that are long gone but had a major impact on my life. I rode through the projects that were one block behind us called East Gates Projects. They are no different than other cities' government assisted housing. So many children are born and raised in these living conditions. Some see the things that go on in them and strive to do better and get out, others embrace what they learn and continue with the negative behavior throughout their life. It was a long time before I was allowed to go to Eastgate because there was so much going on there i.e. (gambling, drugs, prostitution, murder, etc.) So many now from Eastgate are dead and gone, a lot of them that I grew up with and went to school with. I get phone calls all the time letting me know that this one was killed or that one. It's just a sad never-ending story, but I will never ever forget where I came from, because along with all the bad, much knowledge, wisdom and love came from Dark Hollow. The people of Dark Hollow didn't have much, but they had much to give. What they gave of themselves was more than material things, and I absorbed it all. Some of the lessons taught me what I needed to know to not get caught up in the bad things going on all around me, so I am grateful for those lessons also. Most of the elderly residents are no longer there, but the tradition of knowing who is when it comes to Dark Hollow has never changed.

MAKE YOUR FAMILY PROUD

Make your family's name stand out with whatever you do. When your cousin, nephew, grandson or whichever family member it may be, decides to have a party, your name should be the first name on the guest list, because that shows that they are proud of who you are and/or what you have accomplished. Their invite means that they honor and respect you. Many relatives will be jealous; don't get upset with them, just let them know they can do the same. They can take that negative energy and apply it to themselves, by finding their talent. We can all ask God to guide us throughout our life and show us our purpose in life.

VALIDATION

Everyone likes a compliment or validation. If it's a handsome man or pretty lady, they want to be told. When you are in track, you want to be told you ran a great race. When you draw a pretty picture of birds, you like to hear that it is a very nice drawing. Kids especially like to hear they did a great job on their report card. When you can give a great speech, you want to be validated. I have learned that it's not just individuals, but animals also appreciate being rubbed on the head when they fetch the ball or do something right. Validation encourages progress. When a grandfather brings a child to a doctor's appointment or barber so that the parents don't have to take off from work, it's not that they are expecting to be paid, but the validation that they get can puts a smile on their face, that money can't buy. Think of the feeling of winning a Superbowl or a state championship and being lifted off the ground by your other teammates. Do not hesitate to use your God given talent, to be the best at whatever you do, and don't be afraid to try. What if Aretha had never sung a song, Muhammed never started boxing, B.B. King or Elvis never picked up a guitar? I'm sure at some point, Ray Charles and Stevie Wonder, because they couldn't see, were told they weren't going to make it because they were blind, but there were so many others that believed in them and told them to pursue their dreams. That encouraged and validated them, and looked at what they became. Maya Angelou experienced so many setbacks in her life; she may have never thought about writing poems, and she would have lived with regrets. There are famous cooks in the culinary world, renowned barbecue cooks, bakers, pastry chefs, all with histories that prove you can be whatever God has gifted you to be, or whatever you want to be. Don't be good, be great, don't just be a piano player or a person that sings or runs track, be great at what you do. Always finish the job, don't quit. People will always remember a person that finishes the job; they will forget a quitter, but they always remember the person that finished. When I ran track in junior high school, I saw a racer that people laughed at and made fun of. It was a two-mile run and fifty people took off running. In this race, all the people pretty much lapped this young Caucasian runner about three or four times, but he never quit. At one point, the track meet was held up because of him, but he took his time and even though people were laughing, he kept running. I said to myself, '*What a conqueror.*' I found out that there are two kinds of conquerors: one who is a conqueror and one who is more than a conqueror: a story says that there is this hill in a certain country, and the mountain is so steep that if you climb all the way to the top, they raise your hands and say you are a conqueror. Then they make you go down and put a weight on your back and if you make it back up, they say that you are more than a conqueror. This story puts me in the mind of black people; we are more than conquerors. No matter how much weight you put on us, we don't stop. We keep going. I am truly proud to be a black man; I can hold my head up high and say that there is no shame in being a black man. I tip my hat off to all black men and tip my hat off twice to all black women, because I have many black women in my life that have taken care of home and responsibility as if it was easy, but we know it was hard. You saw them sweat, but never weak. Black women to me are the most precious thing. They know how to keep a home and children clean and respectful, and a real black woman will stand up for herself, even when she knows she can't win. You can call her ugly, bald headed, bad built, whatever, she might think for a moment, but she knows she's beautiful. Black, skinny, tall or poor, a black woman has beauty within her that you can't see or touch.

BE CAREFUL WITH MONEY

Please be careful with money; the bible says for the love of money is the root of all evil. Please be careful with how you think about money. Money has destroyed so many women, men, boys and girls. It has caused family members to kill and fight each other and has broken up happy homes due to not having enough coming in or too much going out. If money is not handled right, it can affect your entire attitude about a person. For example: Taking loans from people that are willing to help you, and then because you can't pay them back like you agreed, you stop answering their calls or continue to make excuses about why you can't pay them. If a person does something for you like lend you money, especially if you were in a bind, they shouldn't have to keep calling you asking for their money. When you owe a person, it is simple, pay them their money. Put yourself in that person's shoes. They might have loaned you money that they were saving to pay a bill that they knew they had coming up and expected that you would be a person of your word and pay them when you agreed. Now you have caused a problem in that person's life because they wanted to help you. The Bible says 'Do unto others, as you would like done unto you.' Don't go around having to run and hide from people because you owe them money. Have a word, you never know when you might need them or someone else again, and now the word is out that you can't be trusted with money, and you lose a relationship that was important in your life. Sometimes winning money will cause you to become an arrogant person. You gain 'so called' friends and lose the real ones. Your circle changes, maybe because you feel that you are now more important than the people who were in your circle or the people in your circle now become jealous. Suddenly, people are looking for you, waiting for you to come around. Be careful of these friends because the moment you lose all the money, those friends will also be gone I dare you to try it. When you have money, you'll go to the club, and everyone will be calling your name; they will be complimenting you on the nice car you are driving and all the women will want to be with you. The phone will be constantly ringing and if your name is Greg, you become Big Greg, if your name is Pam, you become Big Pam, but the moment you lose the money, things and people change. My friend's favorite words are "I've seen the loud get quiet when the money is no longer there, be careful."

TRUST AND PRIDE

Trust is something that doesn't come overnight; trust is something that comes with time. Husbands and wives that don't trust each other will find themselves constantly having issues in their marriage. However, trust can sometimes seem as if it takes a lifetime to develop. Trust can only be earned, not bought, but once you are able to find trust, it takes so much pressure off your relationships. It's like a finger with a pus bump, once it bursts, the pressure is released. We as a black community have lost trust for one another; there is not even trust in the churches. That's one of the reasons that we don't support each other and that sometimes we don't visit family. I would like to know how we can get the trust back. Once a person has betrayed you, it's hard to give them a second chance. You may ask, "Why should I trust you again?" The reality of my question is, God says he forgives 70 times 70, and this world is built off mistakes and failures, but people have to see a difference in what you have done in the past and what you are doing now. For a change, if you visit a picnic, even if you have nothing to bring, come early and help set up. People will see a change in who you are becoming. I think it is especially important that you let them know you apologize for your past actions. Once they believe you are truly sorry, in time, the trust can be restored.

I found out that a black man has a million dollars' worth of pride. I 've never been anything but black and carry that same type of pride. However, I'm beginning to see that much of that black pride is in the cemetery, hospital, homeless, or in prison or it just walked out of divorce court. Some people have so much pride that they can't go to momma's house on her birthday or Thanksgiving because they don't feel that they can go as a star or celebrity, or they haven't accomplished enough. Because of pride, some people aren't willing to take responsibility for their actions; they won't admit that they have done wrong. Many of you could probably fix your marriage if not for pride. Sisters and Brothers, you can learn how to talk to each other if it wasn't not for your pride. You might still have your best friend or job if it was not for pride. Pride is dangerous to hold on to. Don't let pride keep you miserable for the rest of your life, let it go. Your word and a handshake should be your bond.

FORGIVENESS & MISTAKES

One of the main reasons blacks hold on to pride is because we don't feel that the person will forgive us. If I thought you would believe me, I would apologize, and why should I have to apologize first? We must have a forgiving spirit. God says there is no sin greater than the sin of unforgiveness. We live our lives out in 'you slap my child, I slap yours'. We must strive to all be in a forgiving mode at all times. Forgiveness can mend relationships. Once you ask for forgiveness, you start talking about having fun, laughing and joking; once the forgiveness is reciprocated, both parties can start over and put the issue behind them. Some people may say they will forgive, but they don't. They won't invite you over, but once you forgive, they not only invite you over, but they also come by and pick you up. Remember forgiveness goes both ways; you and the person both must forgive. You can't keep recalling what happened in the past every time you find yourself disagreeing.

At the age of fifty-five, I can tell you that you will make so many mistakes by the time you reach fifty that you won't be able to count them, but that's okay, because mistakes should make you better. If you walk in a field and run into a snake, you should not stay on the path. Not that snakes aren't on the other path, but at least now, you know where they are in the grass. You should learn from mistakes and avoid making the same mistakes repeatedly.

FAITH AND BELIEF

My grandmother said faith without belief is dead, you got to believe in something and believe by faith that it will come to pass; and that goes with whatever you are trying to do in life. A beautiful young lady or young man can think of faith like wanting to be asked to a dance. You must have faith that you will be asked, but also you must make a way for the person you want to know it. The person may be shy or something, but they go to the dance with just their friends. You can still exercise some faith. Guys if you ask a girl for a dance, you must believe she will say yes. If you want to earn a degree, you must believe in yourself enough and say to yourself that you are going to walk across that stage. You must exercise faith in your companion and your children. Show them you trust they will make the right choices. Speak positively to them about whatever they are trying to do.

FAMILY AND FRIENDS

Relationships are so weak nowadays. For one thing, grandmothers and grandfathers are gone, brothers and sisters are fighting, cousins are like strangers, uncles are on drugs and/or alcoholics, and aunts have more problems than they can handle. Most families aren't carrying the torch. We used to eat at grandmother's house on Sundays and the Preacher, neighborhood or anyone without food was welcomed at my grandmother's table because there was always more than enough. God was always blessing the big mamas to help feed everyone and keep the neighborhood together. The family that prays together stays together. Today we are like aliens in our family. Walking, reading what social media says and not sitting at the table eating together. We don't spend quality time together. When a man and /or woman allows this to happen in their home, the devil will take over because there is no structure, or foundation. Where have our families gone?

I look at the friends I have in my life and have learned how to start classifying all of them. I believe that in life, you may have childhood friends, college friends and religious friends in church that you meet. All the other people are what you call podners, buddies, road dogs, so-called friends, but real friends will know just as much about you as you know about you. Childhood friends you might have been sweet on or loved to play with. College friends you talked with about your future, your grades, maybe even the results of a college girlfriend's pregnancy test. Your college friend may be someone you go shopping for furniture with, someone you feel you can trust with your information and secrets. A church friend may be someone that you can talk about 'getting married' to, how many kids you plan to have. After you and your church friend have been saved, the level of their responsibility to you changes. They will stop you from drinking, clubbing, smoking weed, will ask you to go to bible study, get you prepared for the first marriage. They might ask questions about the woman you have chosen for a wife. *Does she go to church, does she cook, does she respect you/others, what do you have in common, are you able to communicate with her?*

You must be very careful to separate friends, partners, and buddies. That favorite person that you have in your life should only be one and that's the one called your best friend. People don't understand that this person knows more about you. They can hurt you and help you, either way. A so-called friend is one that will be with you today and tomorrow they will be with someone else. Tomorrow you might hear the story about what you did the night before, and they might not tell the whole story or the whole truth about what happened. When this happens, you must remember who and what they are to you. The one that will hurt you the most is that best friend you have shared a lifetime with. The one that you have shared weddings, funerals, graduations and some have changed your kids' diapers with. That same one will be the one because they know you the most.

DON'T RUSH, TAKE YOUR TIME

While in high school, most of my college buddies had their own apartments, cars, and money. I would say I couldn't wait to have my own. How I wish I could take those words back: "Be careful what you pray for, you have plenty of time to be grown." Many unwanted children are born, men are in prison, and some are using alcohol and drugs because they are moving too fast and running with the wrong crowd. Automobile accidents and wrecks happen often because of speeding, wanting the fast life, and being in a hurry because you think you are going to miss something. So many people need patience. Even when taking a test, driving, or deciding which college to attend, take your time.

DISTRACTION

People don't talk about distractions; they keep it on a hush, but half are dealing with people who try to tell them how and what to do. I tell people to ask God to guide them, allow Him to minister to them, and give them guidance on what to do and how to do it. What's for you is for you; advice from other people is okay, but they don't know what God has for your life. You can come to a standstill because you have too much information, and trying to decide which information is right for you can cause problems and confusion. You can make the wrong decisions and eventually realize you went to the wrong college, enlisted in the wrong branch of the military, didn't take a job you liked because people told you about the problems they encountered, or missed a good relationship because you listened to what someone said about the person that you were interested in. My friend told me this, and my cousin told me, "Don't be distracted." Sometimes it's too late when a person realizes they could have left town and bettered their life, only to end up with regrets because they paid attention to all the distractions around them.

DO THE RIGHT THING

With everything you do in life, the load can be lifted if you do the right thing. I have done wrong by people and couldn't sleep, couldn't face that person, didn't know what to say to them if I accidently bumped into them in the street somewhere. Do the right thing. What is the right thing to do? Don't steal from anyone, don't tell lies, don't be an arrogant person, don't be mean and hateful to others. Do the right thing and help others whenever you have a chance.

THE FUN OF BEING BLACK

Black people are natural entertainers, fun in nature, love to laugh and joke and love to dance. There is nothing like passing on the street and seeing a few guys singing around a burning barrel, seeing the family's favorite uncle dancing at the barbecue, or having a good game of spades, dominos or checkers. There is nothing like seeing grandparents dance to their favorite song, telling old stories about family members that may longer be here, seeing adult best friends coming for a visit and going out at night dressed like back in the day or seeing single moms with kids on Sunday at the park with sandwiches. All of those were fun days in my life. I remember family holiday gatherings, barbershops, being down at the juke joint, and as kids playing outside at the water hose because there was no pool, my uncle washing the cars, and being careful to make sure the Caucasianwalls were clean of any dirt. It costs way too much to have fun now. Borrowing a cup of sugar was okay then, but now you get talked about if you ask the neighbor to borrow an important ingredient that you forgot to add to your grocery list. It was an honor to hear someone's momma ask if she could borrow a cup of sugar, rice or flour, even though you knew you would never get it back, but now, we don't want to help others, not even our neighbors. We want God to bless us, but don't want to bless others. Even those that have a little more than they need, people don't want to help those that don't really have anything.

MUSIC

Gospel, Blues, R & B, Jazz, Hip Hop. When it comes to music, I thank God for every person, race, and color. It doesn't matter who it was that contributed their writing, singing and all other skills, musical instrumental playing, different instruments, their talent has made a difference in lives. Gospel music is very inspirational and unique. The words move you and some of the testimonies in the songs give you hope, strength and patience. Some of my favorite gospel artists are James Cleveland, Aretha Franklin, Mahalia Jackson, The Winans and Shirley Caesar just to name a few. The people that wrote these songs got you over the hill, river, and mountain. R&B is what kept me sustained as well. Love songs by the O'Jays, Barry Caucasian, Temptations, Stephanie Mills, Anita Baker, Gladys Knight and Natalie Cole, made you want to have a date to dance with, someone to call yours. Talking on the phone, while listening to these songs helped with your conversation (rap). Then it came to the Funkadelics, Parliament, Bootsie, Earth, Wind, & Fire, Zapp, Roger Troutman, Ohio Players, Commodores & Cameo. When it came to the blues, I considered it to be a national anthem for blacks, because we were often sad because we were lost, because we couldn't get something, and the blues reflected what we were going through. Some of the legends of blues music are BB King, Bobby Bland, Betty Wright, James Brown, Michael Jackson, Prince, legends of all music. I also enjoyed Dolly Parton, Loretta Lynn, the Judds, Roy Clark, Conway, Willie Nelson, Lawrence Welch, Johnny Cash and Elvis. The Hip Hop music industry has its giants also, Mary J, Salt and Pepper, Madonna, Cindy Lauper, Tina Marie, Ice Cube, LL Cool Jay, TUPAC, Mystical, Snoop Doggy Dog, all those including MC Hammer, have impacted my life and everyone has their list. I look around at people at festivals, and I can safely say, music unites people. Whenever you need to make a trip or have a situation in your life, you can find your favorite song to listen to and it can make it alright.

GET YOUR KIDS A JOB EARLY

Even if it's a lawn mower job, I think it's very important that a young man or woman be introduced to what money does. If you introduce them to money, it shouldn't drive them. They should be able to make it and use it to better themselves and open doors to their future. I was introduced to money when I turned eight for my birthday. My great grandfather gave me a twenty-dollar bill. I thought I was rich. I went to the store to buy candy, honey buns, and still had money for the week. I made up my mind that I wanted twenty-dollar bills all the time. I loved my twenty-dollar bills. My great grandmother had me do something on a Saturday morning that changed my life. She said after breakfast that I needed to cut the grass. I didn't know how to work a lawn mower, but I knew how to work a push mower and at eight, I cut it and she smiled. She told me you did a good job and she asked if I could cut the back. Before I could go to the back, my neighbor across the street, who was seventy-seven years old, asked if I felt like cutting her yard and I said, "Yes Ma'am, as soon as I finish with the back I'll come." Then Ms. Green asked if I had time for one more and I said, "I sure do." I had another twenty-dollar bill, each. That's all I talked about was the twenty-dollar bills I had collected that day, and I said, "I'm going to cut some more yards tomorrow and I'll have more twenty-dollar bills." I asked another neighbor about cutting her grass the next day, but my grandmother said, "No. Not tomorrow, it is Sunday. We don't cut grass on Sunday, it's the day we go to church, and it's a rest day, you can cut more on Monday." I cut Uncle Richard's, Aunt Edna's and others. I was eight years old asking my mother's friends, Ms. Randolph, Preacher Barnett, Mr. Rogers and before I knew it, I was an entrepreneur. I had about fifteen yards to do every two weeks. After finishing yards on my street, I went to the Caucasian side of town across the bridge. Blacks on one side, Caucasians on the other. I would get up early, eat breakfast, tie my gas can to the lawnmower and head to the gas station to fill the gas can. I would push the lawnmower to the Caucasian side of town, at eight years old knocking on doors. I was afraid, but I continued because I found out the value of a twenty-dollar bill and I was successful. Five older Caucasian ladies looked forward to me cutting their yards every two weeks, one hundred dollars every two weeks. That was how I bought school clothes and had fun with friends. I felt bad as I left older Caucasian ladies' houses because they would offer me tea, cookies and sandwiches, but I didn't know them, so I turned them down. Because I knew about racism and prejudice, I wondered how they felt about me not accepting their offers. Either way, I cut grass until I was thirteen or fourteen years old because I had so many things, I wanted to buy that my mother couldn't afford. Because of my hustle, she wouldn't have to buy clothes, shoes or anything I needed to go to school, and I wanted to go to school looking sharp. I bought my first guitar player and amplifier myself.

I was taught how to take care of the lawnmower that my grandfather bought me; it was green and black. My great grandmother showed me how to take care of my clothes, how to iron and hang them on hangers; she also taught me how to brush my teeth and about hygiene. At first, I would only brush my front teeth and she said what about those in the back. People would say, "You have pretty Caucasian teeth" and I would say, "I brush them enough." She also taught me how to run my bath water and sit in the tub to soak because I was always cutting grass and sweaty. My great grandmother taught me where to wash and how to wash. I thank God that I found out because everyone didn't get those instructions. The first time I used mouthwash, I almost choked. I liked it when I was introduced to Listerine because I liked the way it left your mouth feeling, all fresh inside after you spit it out. She also taught me to put shoes together under the bed and to take a warm towel and wipe my tennis shoes off. My mom also spoke to me about hygiene and fashion. My great grandmother had a whatnot shelf that me and my sister would scrub clean. We would take a tub of hot water and put all the whatnots in it, wash them and dry them. We then had to dust the shelf by spraying it with Pledge and shining it. We learned to do chores that would help us be responsible when we are older, and the experience has stayed with me to this day. I learned that you must get your children to respect you, early. My grandparents would say "you better straighten your face before I give you something to frown for." One of my mom's favorite sayings was 'do you understand me?' She always closed with this saying. You could never say you didn't understand her.

WHY DO BLACK PEOPLE STEAL?

Many black people won't admit that they have stolen something, but I will admit that I have stolen things before.

I stole because I went so many times without things other people around me had that I didn't. I was sick of tired of being sick and tired. My mother worked two jobs to keep a roof over our heads, to pay bills, buy groceries and gas, the necessities and we never went hungry or homeless. However, when it came to things like fancy clothes, shoes, sports, games and other school events, my mother didn't have the extra money for us to have these things. I, however, thought I should've had them, especially because I saw other families having more than us. As a kid, getting a new pair of tennis shoes was like getting a car. I didn't want to wear my new tennis shoes. I just wanted to look at them. I would sit them on the bed and stare at them, because I didn't want to get them dirty. I would put them to my face to smell the newness. My mother would ask, "Where are the new shoes?" I would say, "They are in the room." I eventually wore them after a week, and I found out that there was another boy named Lawrence Davis, III, in my class who was jealous that I had gotten the new shoes. He stepped on my new tennis shoes on purpose, and he had on tennis shoes that were dirty. I looked at my shoes and there was a muddy print on them, causing me to get really upset because he did it on purpose. After he stepped on them and saw the print he had left, he said, "They are not new anymore." I realized everyone in the first grade was saying *Marvin got new tennis shoes* and he couldn't take it because he didn't have any, so that's why black people steal, because we have been so long without nice things and when others see us finally get something better than them, they want to destroy it. My first bike was stolen from me. I saw it later and my mom talked to the 'kid that stole the bike's parents. His parents asked, "Why did you steal this little boy's bike?" He said he wanted one. I knew how it felt to want something that someone else had, and you knew you wouldn't be able to have it. I felt so bad about his dad saying how he would whip him. I wanted him to have the bike. It didn't mean the same to me anymore. We have stolen because we feel *if someone has it, why can't I.* We don't want to be left out; we want to feel special. If someone steals our shoes, hats, clothes or money, then we will do what we can to try to replace it. We don't want to be left out, we want to have fun too, to laugh and play. I have seen people steal people's coats at school. You were considered special if you had a nice coat or nice jewelry on. We steal for the same reasons people rob banks. Because they are tired of being broke. There are some things I said I'd never steal such as food or any of my friends' girlfriends. I have some friends that I have watched do it though. Back in the day, one reason I had vowed to never steal food was because I wasn't lacking in that area. One day at the grocery store, a black lady was caught stealing and she was brought back into the store and made to empty her jacket and pants. The owner asked, "Why are you stealing?" She said, "Because we don't have food and money for me and my kids." The manager was going to call the police, but when she said what she said, he shook his head and bagged the groceries and asked her if there was anything else she needed. He told her to go get a buggy and get some other things. He went on to say, "But don't come back stealing, if I'm here, come find me and I will help you." My childhood friends, on the other hand, sometimes stole things for fun. I learned a lesson from the lady at the grocery store, *ask people for what you want.* I knew friends that would steal so much, I used to think it was a hobby for them. I even saw them steal from their mother's purse; I've never done that. In summary, people steal because they have been without for too long. Most Caucasians don't understand it, but us blacks would sometimes wear each other's clothes like shirts as youngsters in order to seem to get new clothes or have different clothes.

WHY DO BLACK PEOPLE LIE

Black people lie to cover up life situations. I learned to lie early. I didn't like it, but I didn't want to be embarrassed. I remember my second-grade teacher. Before class started, she would have everyone stand, say their name, and tell what we did for the summer. I would be number three or four in my row; there were two Caucasian kids ahead of me. One said they "went to Virginia to see grandma." The other went to Disneyland, then a black girl hunched her shoulders. The teacher asked her again; she didn't know what to say to the teacher, so she said nothing. The teacher asked her again, "Well tell us what you did?" She said, "I told you that I didn't do anything." When it was my turn, I was so scared that I couldn't tell the truth. I had to say something. So, I said, "Well we did a lot, we took a family trip to Dog___ patch USA, and rode rides, big rides, and games. I also went to California to visit my cousins; I did have some there, but I had never been there." Then I said, "I did more." The teacher knew I was lying, she said "Marvin more?" I said, "Yes, Aunt Jennie Mae who lives in Detroit Michigan sent for me and my sister to come on an airplane ride to see her." I needed to tell that story too. Everyone said, "Wow! Marvin, you had a great summer." I never went anywhere, but all the kids wanted to be my friend. People will judge you sometimes if you tell the truth. We lie to not be trapped with shame, to cover hurt, embarrassment and to get people to look at us differently. It worked for me. A lie sometimes cometh firsthand in a relationship. I have come to find out everyone has lied, and I will say some will still lie today. Some people tell so many lies, they start to believe the lies. So many lies have gone to the grave. There are so many people sitting behind bars, convicted by a lie, whereas some people have gotten off by lying. We see prisoners get out after forty years for something they didn't do because the system found someone else to blame by and saying they fit the description. Now I will say I am guilty of this. Some of the biggest liars tell women what they want to do for them and what they will do when they get them. Most men will lie to get what they want. Some people are forced to lie, and some are bribed. Lying has been around a long time, but I'm at the point where I don't lie about things anymore. I've learned it's disrespectful. As a man, I don't have to tell a lie even though it might hurt; I've practiced telling the truth, it's called being a grown man, a man of integrity as well. I will not lie about anything, not even when I'm broke and need to borrow money. People say, "I will pay you Friday," no, I'll pay you when I get it, but I'm not going to lie. There comes a time when we put foolish games away and be real, be a man or a woman.

CHEATING

Cheating is dangerous, and people often get hurt. Some have even been killed because of cheating. I've seen people get hurt gambling, behind playing poker and cards. Cheating in relationships, telling someone that they are your partner, knowing that you have someone else or more than one or even married is just disrespectful. Sometimes you cheat thinking that you won't get caught because you are across town cheating, but they don't have to see you; they have friends, relatives and enemies that can't wait to destroy you, so they will say they saw so and so with someone else. "*I thought they were married.*" It may take a while, but cheating never pays off. I hate it, because when you get caught cheating, lying and being low down, that look is the most miserable. Not getting that job promotion you knew you should have gotten because you are caught cheating on your hours at work is just karma waiting to happen. You want to laugh or play it off, but you can't run when you are caught cheating. Many people cheat themselves. You might ask how this happens. For example, you worked hard, and you want to buy shoes, cars or a nice place, but you're living in moms house, won't cook dinner and eat a sandwich to keep from buying food, won't buy furniture, you go as far as to avoid grooming, or taking a trip because you are cheating yourself, even when you have money. Sacrificing for the greater good is fine, but not when it comes to diminishing your standard of living when you have the resources to at least get yourself groomed or a healthy meal. We cheat ourselves, and God I am guilty of that. We cheat our parents because we feel that if they don't ask us for anything, they don't need anything. You may think *they don't want to go anywhere; she is just sitting around the house.* What makes you think this? They are still breathing; they still need to wear shoes. We will offer to take everyone else on a trip, but not Mom and Dad. Even though they really want to go, they don't want you to go out of your comfort zone by saying they really want to go. Why can't you just go by and tell them, "Come let's go for a ride." Cheating is a dangerous game that will catch up with you.

SPELLING

Spelling was hard because I did not read enough. At fifty-five, it's still hard because I don't spell very well. I can read it on paper, but don't ask me to spell it. Spelling is important, you will need it. My first real girlfriend in the seventh grade asked for a love letter. I told her I didn't write love letters. She did, and I loved the way it felt to get that first love letter from someone you care about. She would ask daily when she would get a love letter. However, because my spelling and my handwriting were so bad, it kept me from writing the letter that she really wanted. I didn't want to lose her, so one day, I picked up the paper and began writing, but I balled it up seven or eight times and threw it in the trash. Finally, I wrote a small paragraph, and she loved it. I found that it is the thought that counted with her. I achieved something that I thought I couldn't do. Sometimes a little push can make you achieve something that you thought you couldn't do.

COOKING

I'm ashamed to say that I just learned to cook at fifty-one years old. Until then all I knew how to cook was hamburgers, hot dogs, bologna and breakfast. I have tried to barbecue for over thirty years and just got it right. I have burned and overcooked enough meat until I finally got it packed. One of my favorite dishes is baked chicken, country style ribs, fried cabbage, pinto beans and cornbread. The first time wasn't the best, but it turned out pretty good. Every man should know how to cook for his kids, wife and loved ones. Just like us men, a woman also appreciates coming home and dinners done. Shame on you waiting for your wife to cook. Daughters and kids need assistance, and we need to help them. Your sons and daughters should learn to cook breakfast for the family. Daughters should at least learn to prepare cakes, pies, meatloaf, candied yams, macaroni and cheeses. Sons should at least know how to barbecue. Know it well because it is like a job buying meat, seasoning the meat, marinating the meat, cleaning the grill, knowing what charcoal to use, knowing how to light the fire, when to flip meat, what temperature to cook the meat and when to take it off. Your son and daughter should be able to do what you taught them, at least as good or better than you taught them. I would be proud of my sons. When it comes to cleaning, it started at home with my mother. You had to make your bed, fold clothes, put your shoes in the closet side by side like in the military. She didn't play. There could be no paper on the floor, no paper underbed, dishes had to be clean, and the tub, commode and sink had to be clean. Every week my momma taught me important things like how to wash clothes for the first time. I mixed all kinds of clothes before she taught me and I learned how to fold towels, but I do like washing dishes but not sweeping, even though I don't mind vacuuming, and don't be offended, it's just me. I thank God for the two men that raised me. John Shelton and Johnny O'Bryant. I am also grateful for my uncles Charles O'Bryant, Wealthy O'Bryant, Larry O'Bryant and William Bill Tabron. These men taught me so much I could never explain it. My Aunt Hazel Tabron was an All-American aunt. She's one of a kind, a legend in her own time. My grandmother Rosie Lee O'Bryant was the greatest grandmother in the world. She taught me about how a young man is supposed to be and about God. She also taught me about reading the Bible. She read it to me and taught me how to pray. She was like fine wine to me. My mother Erma Lee O'Bryant is the greatest mother in the world, sweetest lady in the world, but don't cross her. She didn't mind taking it to the street. My utmost respect and love go to her, and words cannot express what she means to me. The love she has for people is unbelievable; when God made her, he broke the mold. I love my siblings, my sister Debra Shelton English and my brother Dwayne O'Bryant. I love my whole slew of kinds, the Gaines, Sheltons, Barnes, O'Bryants, Tabrons and Polks just to name a few. You have been a great inspiration in my life. Special love for my class of 1985 Pine Bluff High Zebras and to the whole Pine Bluff nation; you have been a great blessing to me.

HIDDEN & MIXED EMOTIONS

It's one thing to be caught in emotions, but it's another to hide from them. So many blacks hide behind hidden emotions because we are ashamed for others to know. We don't talk, we keep it hidden, but we are fighting everyday with these emotions. Years go by and some take them to their graves. Emotions are powerful; they are balled up inside and let me say this, when people battle with their emotions, it can leave permanent scars. People for many years wrestle with telling their loved ones their emotional struggles People need to realize that the sooner they let it out the clearer you see and the more we understand. They don't eat at the dinner table and never want to sit with the family while playing games or watching TV, but instead, seem so caught up in what they are doing. When someone asks how they are doing or if they are, okay? They say, 'I'm okay'.   Certain things like being overweight, poor, and being uneducated can truly affect people in different ways. In my day, people who stuttered or were cross-eyed, slew footed, knock kneed, handicapped, walked with a limp, or had one arm shorter than the other were mostly seen or treated differently than their peers, which led to pent up emotions about fitting in. Nevertheless, I found out that time brings change. I have seen it, but some are still stuck even after fifty years, hiding behind emotions... Many other races don't grow up with the emotions that blacks have. Emotions will make you cry a lot, trust me I know, and I understand the key to emotions is to find Hope, find out who you are and be who you are regardless of what others say. You need to be pulled out of emotional stress. Be who you are going to be, do what are you going to do and grab hope; it will pull you up. Remember you are God's child, you are somebody, you have a purpose so don't let emotions take you out. Grab some hope and pray; this is the medicine that helps cure emotions one day at a time.

One of the most disappointing feelings is when your dad hugs and kisses you and says I love you, then promises to buy you a bike and he doesn't. Similarly, when mother would say you can go to the baseball game and change her mind at the last minute, you become devastatingly confused. If your partner says "I love you" but when they go out, they are hanging with someone else, mixed emotions get in. Whether it be politics, a promotion, job, raise or doing any kind of work, you can start to have mixed emotions about the situation. It can become stressful. So many people even have mixed emotions about the bible or religion. God is coming back soon, but people will sit and wonder if He really is going to return and when He is coming back. Sometimes we need to control our emotions and avoid feeding too deeply into things, for our own sake and to avoid getting ourselves stressed out.

KNOWLEDGE

Knowledge rules the world. It's a powerful thing to be able to know facts. People listen because you are telling them something they don't know. Knowledge is power, a lot of Blacks have died because of knowledge, been fired, kicked out during slavery. It was against the law for black men or women to be able to read and write. It hurts my heart to see a person with a lack of knowledge. For the past seven years, I was in transportation. I picked up one woman in her seventies and one in her early sixties who were from a town I have never heard of in Mississippi. The knowledge they were full of was remarkable. One could tell that they had been through some things and had seen a lot. The younger lady started speaking while I was driving, and it brought tears to my eyes. It hurt my heart to know that there are people in their 60s that can't read. To hear her tone made it appear as if she was in the second grade and it took me back to slavery remembrance. Is this the way slaves talked? The English was horrible, so my prayer is that everyone sharpens his or her knowledge. I don't know everything, but I know a little about a whole lot. I watch TV and listen to the radio. The old folks say it's better to need and have than to not have it and need it.

SPORTS

I think that every young black male and female should be pushed to do their best in sports because we are born athletes. We have the muscle and ability to be great in physical areas and everything we touch. We are born with great strength to run, jump and climb; we are competitive and it's easy for us to be good at what we do. With a little training, we can be great. We must push our children to be great. When it comes to professional sports, there shouldn't be another race of people in the pool, on the basketball court, on the football field, on the tennis court, and baseball diamond who can match our skills. We are natural born, talented people. There are great athletes but there are so many natural born athletes in our black community. Long jumpers, high jumpers and boxers; there is nothing we can't dominate with the proper training and be great. Legendary athletes have come through, but there are so many of us that don't get the opportunity because of a lack of support. For example, Mike Tyson had been in trouble all his life, but when Cus D'Amato discovered him (an elderly Caucasian man that took him in as a juvenile), he saw something in him moved Tyson in. Kevin Rooney trained Mike and he became one of the youngest to win the Heavyweight Championship of the World in boxing. After Mike won his first fight, the rest is history. All I'm saying is, recognize natural talent then get the training and support; what a difference it made in his life, thank you, Cus D'Amato.

A PRODUCT OF YOUR ENVIRONMENT

As a product of your environment, when the environment has been bad, like being poor and being raised in the projects, your eyes may have seen the worst things. That doesn't mean that you must remain a product of that life. You don't have to get involved with drugs, you don't have to sell, you don't have to curse because everyone around you is, you don't have to flunk out of school, and you don't have to fight. In my lifetime, I have seen doctors, lawyers, politicians, preachers, and good citizens come out of the worst areas. If you come from a good family and are blessed to have the things you needed while young, keep that torch going, thank God that you didn't have to come up through tough times, and don't do anything to shame your family name, especially when your older family members have worked hard to be respected.

REALITY

Reality is a very powerful word to so many people

including myself. Every human being, if they are living, must face reality. It doesn't matter the color, race or financial standing, reality must come. Everyone has had their own reality ticket. Reality is basically in my eyes a moment that you stop, acknowledge it and speak to it. No one can work out your reality; you must work with it. You must work with what it is and work with God. For instance, *"I woke up black"* is my reality; what I do with this is up to me. I woke up in some poverty- that's reality, I woke up to a broken home- that's reality, I woke up in a certain neighborhood where there were all blacks and that's a reality. Some of things really hit at a young age. Positive things: I woke up with love all around me and the reality of that is that love ran deep in my family, but I had to face the fact that I was faced with challenges as a young man. The reality was, there were certain places, certain neighborhoods, or communities that you shouldn't go to being black. I also faced the reality of knowing I had to look the part when I went certain places to avoid certain judgement in a particular category. I used to hear people all my life says, *"don't get caught walking through that neighborhood after dark, don't get caught playing with that little Caucasian boy,* what is he doing here? Let him go home"*. That was the reality that I faced as a young kid. As kids, my sister and I would get a speech before going into the grocery store from my great grandmother that said, "Don't touch nothing, stay close to me and don't hit the back of my heel with that buggy." Moreover, you had better not act up in the store. These were her instructions and the strongest reality I faced as a young man was finding myself, what I was going to do with myself because growing up black, what we were always asked was *what we were going to be when you get grown?* So, when you said something important, the expression was a little chuckle; "be a policeman" because the black people back then didn't think it was possible. I wanted to be an attorney, or a doctor they laughed, but the real reality is, it was possible, but sometimes your relatives and parents don't believe in you.

There was a time when the reality for me was that I needed a father in my life, but he seemed like he wasn't coming. I looked for him to come, I sent a prayer for him to come, but he never came. Thank God at fifty, I was allowed to embrace him. Reality works in mysterious ways. Many of us grow jet black hair, no gray, no mustache, no beard. I'm not ashamed to tell you that sometimes I would take my mother's eyebrow pencil and draw a mustache, but the reality is, I have a full mustache now and have to cut it off every week. The reality is I started out as a young boy climbing trees, jumping ditches. I ran fast and I thought I could lift the world. I never felt like anything was too heavy for me, as if I could handle anything. I lived by bringing it on. The reality is, at fifty-five just getting out of bed is a job. All the fast running is no more, when you walk to the house from the car, you feel pain here and there; you go to the store to buy shoes that are comfortable, and maybe not as attractive. I used to worry about name brand shoes, the color, who they were made by, but my new reality is, I just need them to be comfortable. Another reality is that I have zero tolerance for nonsense. Loud music, cursing, grandchildren, nieces, and nephews talking back, being disrespected, riding all over town with friends, clubbing and drinking. Now I realize the things I used to love to do, I don't have the desire to do those things anymore, so therefore, the biggest reality of all that I had to face was growing old, looking in the mirror at myself, because that mirror will always tell you the truth. Another reality I must face is death. Losing loved ones is a very hurtful thing in the black family. It is hurtful in all families, but I say the black family because we hold on to our loved ones strongly because they are all we have. I have been to Caucasian race funerals and the funeral is pretty much conducted like a black funeral, but it's a different vibe. Four or five people may cry because they are missing their loved one, but when it comes to a black person's funeral, we take it personally. We never want to face the reality of death in our families. Another big reality we face is watching our babies grow up and having babies. While all people face the reality of bills accumulating, most black families don't get to prepare for this properly as most times, we lack access to a certain level of qualifications, and it is difficult to acquire fulfilling jobs that allow us from working multiple jobs to cover them. Reality is real and we must respect it.

YOUR WORTH

You must ask yourself *what is your worth?* If I have to say so, everyone is worth millions, if not billions of dollars. Some of us are stuck and do not realize we are worth hundreds and thousands of dollars. As black people, we should face the reality of how much we are worth and not let people put a price on your worth. You must make the decision and you must know for yourself that you are worth millions and billions. If you're going to be a doctor, nurse, architect, lawyer, teacher, plumber, mechanic, barber, or whatever your gift or talent may be, you must make up your mind that you are going to be the best you can be and take it to the next level. There's more to your gift than just working. Even if you have a gift, you must read books about your gift to see what other people with the same gifts have done. At all times, educate yourself. Learn all you can about your gift so that once you master it, whatever it is, no one can just come along and give you anything. People must pay you for what it's worth, whatever price you put on it. That is how some friendships and relationships get messed up. Friends and family always want you to use your gifts to help them and won't pay you. Why is it that they feel that you should work for free? You have bills to pay, you have a family to feed, you want to buy nice things and you may have a car note to pay. When you stop doing it for free, they go and willingly pay someone else and then fall out with you. Pay people for their worth. I feel that is using a person, and you don't want this done to you.

I love to use this analogy when it comes to a woman. Know your worth, and don't just settle for a man because he is cute or has a fine car. Know your worth because all those material things that you fall in love with will fade away one day. The reason that some people stay in poverty is because we don't think we are worthy of better. We accept our situations. I had to say to myself I'm worth more than this, I'm better than this, I deserve better than this; I never accepted my situation. Though I come from a single parent home and a generation of people that were brought up poor, I knew that I would not stay in that bracket. There were so many days that I would be broke and didn't have a dime in my pocket, but I didn't look like it. I didn't walk like it, and I didn't talk like it. People used to think I was rich, but they just didn't know I smiled on the outside all the time but hurt on the inside. I wanted to be somebody, so I was determined to work hard so that I could have a better life than the one laid before me and by the grace of God, I did.

BELIEVE

Believe in yourself. I believe that I can be anything I want to be whatever it is, I believe that I can do it. It's never too late to get off the couch, get out of bed, and do it. Judge Mathis went to prison as a black man and became a judge. I didn't think anyone could do that, but there are all types of computers and classes in jail that can help you achieve a dream. You must believe. When you put belief and faith together, you can't be stopped. I'm a witness that one doesn't work without the other. Most of all, prayer added to that makes the sky the limit. The world is yours, believe me. I had prayer, faith, and belief, and those things took me many places in this life. I have met all kinds of people. I've shook hands with some of the best, so I can thank God for giving me the opportunity to know my worth.

IDENTITY

Your identity is who you believe you are, not what others think about you. It is not defined by your worth or by how tall, cute or good looking you may be. Some people may see you in a certain way and may attempt to label or classify you as who they may believe you are; however, you have got to know who you are and believe in the divine wisdom and gift that God has planted in you. Believe that with God, all things are possible, and nothing is out of your reach. Don't let others define you. I remember in high school; we had a football trainer nicknamed Wimpy. He was a kind of heavyset kid as a tenth grader. Well, ten years went by, I came home for homecoming, and saw him, and I said to him, "What's up Wimpy?" He said to me, "That is not my name," with a straight face. I had known Wimpy to be called just that and only that for so long, I really thought he was playing with his comments, but he repeated himself again, with no smile. I apologized to him and said, "I don't know your real name, that's all we ever called you." He then told me what his real name was and from that day on, I called him by his first and last name. There comes a time in your life that you should put away your childish behaviors and let people know who you are and call you that. I gained a new respect for him that day.

WHAT IS YOUR PURPOSE

Your purpose is the one thing that you would do even if you would not get paid for it. It's the one thing that you love, your passion. When you ask God to give you a purpose, He will, and until you figure out that purpose, you will always find substitutes. You must get to the real purpose. God will show us our purpose, if we ask Him.

WHAT ARE YOU TEACHING

I was taught from birth to train up a child in the way that they should go. If you spare the rod, you spoil the child. No meant no, and yes meant yes, and maybe was in between; we might or might not. Treat everyone the way you want to be treated. Be kind, be helpful and mindful of what you say and how you act.

MANNERISM

I was taught to ask for something if I wanted it, even when it's your mother you ask. I was taught to open doors for people, greet people as 'Yes Ma'am, no Ma'am, yes Sir and no Sir.' I was taught to share and so I despise a stingy person. I was taught to give as a kid. Not my toys or my bike, but my great grandmother taught me to give fruits and vegetables especially to the elderly. That task became easy for me, because I liked the response of taking oranges, figs, pears, or sweet potatoes across the street. The people would light up and it made me feel good; even today when people leave my house, I like to give them something: a bottle of cologne, a shirt, tie, a hat, just something. I've been taught to be a giver. I've been taught to respect yourself and others right. Not to curse, not to hit, not to say things to hurt people's feelings. Even now as an older man, I found myself getting into a situation with friends, heated arguments. Sometimes you say some things you really don't mean, and I have to call them back and apologize because that's not what I've been taught and that's not what's in my heart. I have also been taught not to hold grudges against those that use you or do something that blocks your path. I forgive them and I move on. So, I must ask a question, because I see so many women teaching their kids the wrong things and setting bad examples like smoking weed, drinking in front of their kids, dancing in a provocative way, cursing, fighting and some even do drugs in front of their kids. I have seen this with my own eyes. If you are teaching them these things by example, their young minds will pick it up and try it when you are not looking. I remember my first cigarette, first piece of tobacco, my first beer, after my mother had a party and went to work. The next morning, I lit one of those cigarette butts, and whatever beer was in the can, I tried it. It was Garrett Snuff and Beech Nut tobacco that I would get for Uncle Richard and Ms. Georgia. I tried it for myself and oh boy! I got sick at the stomach, dizzy and started to sweat had to go lay down even though it was early afternoon. When my mama got home from work, she asked me, "What was I doing in bed so early?" I told her I was SICK AS A DOG!" It was my stomach and my head". She just turned and walked away. To this day, I still hadn't told what happened that day. So, remember when you plant that seed, it will grow into just what you plant. You must reap it. All young kids are curious and will try things when you aren't looking. I am guilty, because I tried all kinds of things that I saw my adult relatives do when no one was looking. You must be careful what you teach or set an example of, because your kids will grow up and do the same things.

PEOPLE

There are all kinds of people in this world. You must be careful and know what they stand for. Let's start with the mother and father; you must learn to honor and respect them no matter where they are in their life or what they are going through. There is nothing you can change about them. They had a life before they had you. God says you should still honor them. Some might not meet your approval, but they are still on record as your parents. The father may get another family, your mother may divorce and move on, but at the end of the day they are yet due honor and respect.   Mothers and grandparents are your safety nets. They are the ones that usually have their life together, believe in God, trust in God and pray for you. You should see them more settled and doing the right thing. They may not have always been this way, but time brings about a change, so they become a safety net. If you have great grandparents still alive, you are blessed beyond measure. I had the opportunity of being raised by my great grandparents. Having them all alive at one point, I knew God had smiled on me. Having at least one brother and sister is a blessing because no child should grow up by themselves. There will be attitudes, jealousy, and power struggles. There might be fights, but you must always love them and despite things that happen, love them. Uncles and aunts are extra parents. Sometimes they stray off and go on the wrong path, but never turn your back on them. Your cousins, nieces and nephews sometimes may seem to never get on track. You should sit them down and tell them about how to get out of their situations. Outside the immediate family, you will be faced with different kinds of people: some haters, some enemies, some backstabbers, some liars, and some so-called friends.

GRANDMOTHERS

I was raised by my great grandparents and my great grandmother was one of the most precious human beings. It was a blessing to experience my great grandmother's love. My first lesson of obedience, in right and wrong, was with my great grandmother. As mentioned earlier, she taught me "No Ma'am, yes Ma'am, no Sir and yes Sir." It didn't make a difference, everybody that was older than me was Sir and Mam regardless of their skin color. They taught me about being polite, picking up things for others, speaking when being spoken to, learning how to ask questions. They taught me how I should behave in public and showed me that if I didn't behave, when we got home, they had a switch, a back hand, or a look I hated. That look was enough for me to only have to have the back hand once. The switch had to be used a time or two, also. I also learned that money is not everything, sometimes you do things from the heart. I read that old text, *The more you give, the more God will give you.* My grandmother made me read my Bible and taught me how to pray. Her favorite prayer started with, "Our Father which art in heaven." Whenever she got dressed to go pay a bill, she would put on her favorite dress and every hair on her head would be in place. She was a first-class lady, clean, and always sharp as a tack; Mrs. Rosie Lee O'Bryant. She took us to church and praised God. I watched her holler "Yes Lord, praise God." I laughed at her witnessing and raising her hand until she got happy enough to holler. I would just look at her. I learned then that church was not just an organization, it was somewhere to go to let the spirit come in and I wondered about alter call. I would listen to the words, and I would be afraid because if you walked down front some people would assume you had issues and I wanted everyone to think that everything was all right with me. I heard the preacher say, "Bring your burdens to the Lord." It wasn't until I got older, got a few bills, got my own family, and got my own few ups and downs did I learn to take it to the altar. The moral to this story is, you can't be ashamed because we all have ups and downs.

My grandmother was a leader, matriarch and was truly a child of God. She would not have had it any other way. She encouraged us to pray for each other, go to church and worship together even though some of us would fall by the wayside. She made sure we all knew better. Life was not always great, but we knew if we practiced the things my grandmother taught us like gardening, planting seeds, making up the bed, being respectful, treating others right, even when they treated us wrong, we would get a reward. The reward might not be money, but she also taught us that money was not everything. You could tell when my grandmother was especially happy and proud of something we did, because she would make some of our favorite dishes. It might be cake, tea cakes, fried chicken, pinto beans and cornbread, and popcorn balls which were her personal favorites.

BLACK TEACHERS

Thank God for schoolteachers. I will say this about the black ones because they were different. They went the extra mile to ensure that all the students in the class got proper and equal attention as the next person. They did not allow cutting up. We respected them and they made sure we did our homework and understood the lesson. If they were teaching something that they realized we didn't feel comfortable with, they would keep us after class. They usually could tell if there was something on their students' mind and would ask if everything was okay at home. If they felt that our answer wasn't true, they would call our mother or go visit. My black teachers went the extra mile. I remember those teachers; if we were not doing well in their classes, they would try and make sure we could understand our assignments. I've heard them tell young women "Fix your skirt, don't come back to my class with your hair not combed." They went to church with us, were our relatives or they knew the family. I've had counselors, teachers and principals let me know that I wasn't getting away with anything because they knew and had a relationship with my family, and because they knew my family members were a phone call away. I did not enjoy it; if we were messing up, they would paddle us, and we indeed got another paddling when we got home. My black teachers were not afraid of us at all. I knew that all teachers had to be smart, but there was something special about black male teachers; I felt that they wanted to see black children make good grades, to understand the work, advance to the next level and get academic scholarships. They got pleasure in being able to say, "I taught him or her in the fifth grade, tenth grade or even in college." If I knew then what I know now, school is no place to play. You should be eager to run to school even if you miss the bus. We as black students worry about recess, the girls, seeing our friends, when we should have been hungry for more education.

WHITE TEACHERS

One of the reasons I am still writing today is because of my seventh grade Caucasian English teacher. I would love to put my arms around her, because she was the first person that told me to keep writing. She would give us assignments to do, and I would complete them so fast that I knew I had time to do something else, something else like write a song that I had been working on. She would sometimes go to the back of the class to look over everyone and make sure they were doing the assignment. One day, I saw her walking to the back of the class, but I didn't turn around to see how far back she had gone. All sudden, I heard a voice saying over my shoulder, "Who wrote that?" I grabbed my paper scared as she stood over me, because I thought she would destroy it. Once again, she said, "Who wrote that?" I replied, "I did," and she said, "If you keep that up, you will be famous." I felt that I had twenty overcoats on, and they all fell off. I knew I wanted to write songs. I was in a group, and I wrote the songs for our group. I eventually put writing down for sports even though my other teachers had encouraged me that my writing was a gift and that I would do good. They said that my million-dollar smile would take me a long way. At some point, I realized that playing football had become more important to me than writing. I really loved the game and put my all into becoming one of the best football players. Life happened and when I realized I would not be playing any more football, I went into barbering. I really thought I had found my passion in barbering and that I would continue to do it for the rest of my life. As I saw my barbering career coming to an end, I asked God, "What should I do?" He said, "Go back to your first love, writing." I picked up the pen and started writing and it didn't have to make sense. I just scribbled whatever came to mind. So, this is how I restarted my writing journey. Some of my teachers and many of my friends are on Facebook and it touches my heart to see them. I loved some of the Caucasian teachers and they loved my smile. They knew I could do anything that I put my mind to. They loved some of the stories I could come up with and would always call me to the front of the class. My teachers were impactful and showed a true sign of belief in me, so I would like to thank them for their love and concern.

TEARS

I don't think no one has shed more tears than blacks. I can't imagine the tears of slavery. Husbands and wives being sold and raped, so as I come back to now, for so many years we have barely made it. Grandmothers look at their daughters having to move back home because of broken marriages, financial situations, sons being drafted into wars, worried about fighting for their country and not knowing for what. We have experienced sons being beaten while driving, being harassed; the tears of a mother after the father walks out and leaves for another family, then tears of failure depending on the situation. Some have suffered the tears of being falsely accused and doing prison time for something they didn't do. People will have a sickness and no money for a doctor, tears of stress when one has fallen on hard times, but I also learned that there is another set of tears. These are tears of joy. There is nothing greater than a baby being born and raising and pushing that child to do their very best and then witnessing the child getting all A's on their report card, that son making three touchdowns, that grandson's first Easter speech or first steps. The joy of that son coming home for the first time after going into the military, that daughter graduating from college, a niece that is engaged to be married, a grandson being baptized, the uncle that drank every day being finally alcohol free or relatives that are finally drug free, or seeing a divorced couple reconcile. Those are the things that bring me tears of joy.

PRAYER

When I think of prayer, I think it's very important that people understand what prayer can do, what to pray about and how to pray. I was taught at an early age to go to God, and bow my head at the table, get down on my knees raise my hands above my head and just thank God. It shows humility and sincerity. I was taught there is no special time, any time of the day and night daily. I used to pray for just what I wanted when I was in trouble, or sick, but I found out as I got older, I learned to pray when you're doing good and doing bad and most importantly, pray for others, the sick, the loss, and especially your enemies. We must also pray for the neighborhood, town, cities, schools, and the less fortunate. So many people are walking this earth that are lost and need to know about the God that I was taught about. I was taught that God only listens and answers sincere prayer. I was also taught there is no need for long prayer. Sometimes the Lord has mercy, but also understand that when you pray, you must allow God to have His way and His will be done. Once again, I thank God that I found out the meaning of prayer. I urge everyone to take a minute to find out about prayer.

THE BARBER AND THE BARBER SHOP

Ever since I was five years old, the barber shop has been the black man's sanctuary. It's where you saw all the fathers and the black barbers could speak about politics in the town, and city and all the local events that had happened. You could hear it all at the barber if you listened. Back in those days, playing or acting out was not allowed, it was a respectable place. As you came in, you sat down, watched and listened. Johnny O'Bryant, my grandfather would hit the door with five or six of us grandkids; I was amazed at his style, how he joked with people. I must say it has rubbed off on me today. He would come in the shop and say, "Hello to all the women and no men" and the men would say, "Hello" and laugh because no women were in the building. He was that kind of a guy. As a kid, I would wonder about the Caucasian stuff that foamed on their face. My granddaddy would give us change to buy a "pop" and

Lance peanuts. I would mix mine together. Miller's Barber Shop was the place to be, with all the big shots, fancy cars, preachers, with their nice suits on and hats. The men in the shop would get their shoes shined as they waited for their grooming. My experience was watching the shine man, but now you don't see them anymore. I think the most amazing thing was the horning of the razor strap. The barber worked the strap back and forth and then put it on a man's face. Hearing that cracking sound as he did the razor strokes on his face, that was my favorite part, seeing the results of the whole process: a clean-shaven face. In most of the shops, the men played checkers and that was fun to see. No help or anything, mind against mind. I loved to watch the checker game. Back then, there was no TV, so conversation was everything, especially about sports, baseball, and boxing. They would say a little about basketball and a little about football. I must say that if you played close attention, you learned something. I didn't want the haircut because I was afraid of the haircut and all eyes were on me. Even though it was always crowded, it was peaceful; a black man's sanctuary where he could speak his mind because everyone listened to what the other men had to say. When you left, you left feeling full of joy. Then suddenly, out of nowhere, the door would swing open. A big man, six feet five inches, would come into the shop with a big potato sack on his shoulder. He was the Peanut Man. If you had a dime, you would get a hot bag of peanuts. I would wonder how he kept them so hot, and I admired him for getting out and selling peanuts because I understand that his hustle helped put three children through college.

I would love the alcohol that would go around my head, it burned, and we smelled so good. My grandmother would say, "You all smell good." She was very proud. Low and behold, I did not know I would become a barber, but I loved the barbershop and twenty years later, I became a barber myself. For over twenty-five to thirty years of my life, barbering has been my income, my joy, and my love. These two hands have touched the heads of thousands of boys, men and women and I hope I have made them look like they wanted, and I also hope they were able to gain wisdom and knowledge. They were able to hear all the barber talk about my experiences and be a listening ear for them. A barber is a humble man. A barber is also a person that can give you a positive outlook about things you might be going through. Sometimes you can hear some good music that relaxes the mind. Rhythm and Blues will relax you and then you might see a nice young lady bringing her son. All of them would bring their son in looking their best. They would prepare themselves for the barbershop visit because she knew that all eyes would be on her. She would play it down because she knows the barbers are good guys with good sense and knowledge, easy to pick from. If you're reading this book, when you go back home where you are used to getting a haircut from, it's okay to shake the barber's hand and say thank you for the wisdom and knowledge. You can tell him that you appreciate and love him, and he would appreciate it to the utmost. Some people will say the barber is a psychiatrist, doctor, counselor, father figure. As barbers, we say we hold a lot of titles. I'm grateful to be a barber and I'm thankful for the clients; I want to say thank you for the many years of your service and to all the barbers across the globe, I want to say, "Man, I salute you, well done."

BLACK FAMILY REUNION

One of my favorite times was the Gaines Family reunion. It was a very fun time with a big family, probably two hundred people from Wabbaseka Arkansas. How I miss my big family, so many have died, but there are many new ones that I don't know. My first family reunion was at the age of six or seven. I knew about one hundred people that were cousins, but to see the family that had come from Chicago, Denver, St Louis, so many parts of California, Kansas City, Fort Wayne Indiana, and so many other places, I didn't know what to do because there were so many other people I wondered if they really were all my cousins. There were five Gaines brothers; Louis, Levi, Joe, Fred, and Henry. These men left Arkansas and made something of themselves. They were the first ones I looked up to in my family. They drove nice cars and I would light up when they came to town. I could listen to them all tell jokes, and they made me want to be somebody special because they always had time for me. I once heard them talking; each had spent two hundred dollars to make the family reunion work. Now to this day, we still carry on the tradition; almost twenty states out of the fifty gathers for these reunions, but what I admire most of all is how they work together in their backyard. The men would work together in the backyard cleaning and preparing for everyone to arrive as well as preparing the meat. There would be barbecue, fish, and all kinds of sides, which would be prepared by all the women in the kitchen, and we would have eight to ten cold watermelons cut and ready to eat. I never saw them argue amongst each other. All of them believed in marriage, so you saw role models and they all believed in having a good time, you saw unity. Five brothers working together in the same place was amazing and all the cousins that would flow into the yard would be afraid of each because we were young and didn't know everyone, but now after thirty to forty years, we treat each other with much love. Through the years, I am guilty that I don't call enough. It's okay to ask how you are doing; not every day, not every month, just to say, "Hey cousin, I am thinking about you." When we check on each other, a ten-minute conversation might turn into at least two hours. So much has happened since the last time. You need to know who your cousins are. Our kids need to know their family, because you can easily start a relationship without knowing. So be sure to check on your family from time to time.

HURT

The black community is very familiar with hurt. Really and truly, if coached right, we are some of the best actors in the world. We will smile and laugh and be hurt at the same time. We can hold our feelings, hurt and emotions for long periods without bursting. I must say if I was any other race, other than black, I would look back at blacks and ask a question, "How do y'all do what you do? Where do you get the strength? How do you hide it?" Any other race would have lost their minds, committed suicide, gone on a rampage, yet you all have managed to work it out, to keep your sanity. Yea you cried some nights but thank God for His grace and his Word. The Bible has helped us to understand our situations and circumstances; it helped us to manage to walk with our heads held high. Through it all, I've seen black women weep and moan, but I have never seen them give up. I've seen them go on their knees and beg for something that they needed. I've seen black men beg and plead for one more chance, but never have I seen men or women quick to give up. I know God has made us and is with us through all of this. It is my belief that no other animal or human could take this mental, physical, or verbal abuse and still walk this earth, still have a smile or clap his or her hands with joy. Some people may say certain things about how we made it over, but the Bible kept us with sound minds. Therefore, the Bible has been a great book for us to get an understanding of how we all should live. If you are here, living and breathing, you should read the Bible sometimes and get an understanding; it can help you. Though blacks have experienced a lot of depression and hurt, we still move forward. We are unbreakable, we have a higher power that we know, and we must meet our maker, we pray for strength, understanding, vision, patience, wisdom, and He gives us strength and helps us pick our brothers up when they are weak. We are not quitting people. We endure, we are conquerors. It's okay to cry, to weep and groan, but not quit; that's why I'm so proud to be black, because in my living, I've seen this race sing and march on. I've seen them cry as they sing, and I've seen them get stronger. Before you know it, they are wiping away the tears. The more they sang, the stronger they got because they knew they had a purpose to achieve, and they decided to keep marching. There is a passage in the Bible that says *weeping may endure for a night, but joy comes in the morning*. We get up off our knees trusting that tomorrow will be alright and that today is behind us, so we always look forward to a better tomorrow. I must truly say the word of God kept me sustained, hoping, and strengthened in my faith. That's why we start teaching our children young how to have faith. Old people said all you need is a little faith, just as much as a mustard seed. At times, I didn't know what they were talking about, but I found out as I grew older that was really all you needed. Thank God for His word. Without it, we would have perished many years ago. No matter how weak you are, you could still stand up to a giant. Old folks would say if you cut off the head, the body will follow. I feel every black race deserves a mental check. Every black person should not be afraid to see a psychiatrist or psychologist, because there is damage from generations of depression, hurt, being bruised, bitterness, and shame. Many of the black race have had a nervous breakdown and don't know it. You see us smiling, drinking and having fun and wonder why some react the way we do. It is because we are mentally disturbed; mix that with alcohol and drugs and it can become a disaster if that person is pulled over for a traffic stop, already in defense mode. When blacks attempt to ask officers why they pulled them over, the officers act as though blacks don't have the right to know but blacks are tired of being treated like second class citizens and the person that was pulled over got their own problems, financial, physical, emotional, children, a wife and job. Then officers say blacks are resisting arrest. These officers quickly become afraid and hope because of the color of blacks' skin that there is a warrant out for their arrest. Whether there is a warrant or not, it would not be the reason the officer stopped them. Officers know that 60% of black people have some kind of violation on their record. The Officer already knows that there is a 50% chance he's right. We as black people have experience in being black that other people don't have to deal with. We wake up and before we leave our house, we know the possibilities of what we can face and what can happen. We share knowledge, and benefit from events and information that serve or save us. We share when officers are hiding behind bushes, which streets to avoid and when something shady is going down. In America, black men in general don't trust the police. In most cases, they are not our friends and if given the chance, any encounter with them could go the wrong way. We know that once a Caucasian man calls the police, there is a 90% chance blacks are going to jail, even if they are innocent. We have watched the media and have witnessed encounters where Caucasian people have called the police for no reason but the first thing, they do is hear the Caucasian person's side, never want to listen to the black man's side, and we end up in jail. I watched people in the media with cameras going through a sobriety test, they may be nervous from being stopped but, if they are black, it's an automatic failure and off you go to jail. When the officer stops someone black, in some cases, even if they put both hands on the steering wheel, or hang both hands out of the window, the officer will still say the person was reaching for something and might shoot them. I find it funny that the black people pulled over by police are mainly black men not women, and they are young black men. I need to let you know black people have never been dumb. We have had limited access to certain knowledge, but we have never been dumb. We have wisdom and experience, common sense on how to do things; we were survivors when we got here from the beginning. We learned how to hunt in Africa, but when brought us to a strange land, we didn't know how to start. If I brought any stranger to Africa, they wouldn't know how to adapt as well and wouldn't know the language or culture. Again, I thank

God. When I hear people say, "I'm a doctor, I'm a lawyer, I'm an engineer, graduate of this or that institute, I'm a schoolteacher and an architect", it makes me light up with joy when I hear them say that; I think about the cotton field. It makes me light up and say *there is a God.* When I travel and see a two-story house that a black person lives in, it makes me light up and think about LeBron James, Dak Prescott, Michael Vick, Doug Williams. I saw Serna Williams, Venus Williams, and Simone Biles and I still thought about the cotton fields. So being black, I am proud no one gave us anything; we earned and took what we deserved. However, we still haven't gotten a portion of what we really deserve. All the free labor, and women that had those children for their masters never received any child support. There is a lot that I feel we deserve and I'm still waiting on my forty acres and a mule today.

WHO IS TEACHING US?

Who do we have to teach us economics, banking, real estate, entrepreneurship, stocks, bonds, and politics? Who is teaching us the laws of this land, how to be a man? Who is teaching us money, and what to do with our checks that we get on Fridays? It has been said that blacks have been the number one consumer and we spend our income tax and our paychecks before even get it and it leaves our neighborhoods. How to save, how to plan? Black people have so many groups; fraternities, sororities, churches, barber shops and other organizations, but who is teaching us how to cope and get along and build our communities? I didn't get taught. We have the Black Chamber and NAACP nationwide, but are they teaching young people? Are we being encouraged? I think we need to have more encouragement to join fraternities, sororities, and churches. Is the church teaching us the tools we need or is everyone taking from us? I'll be the first to say I made good money, but I didn't know what to do with it. I didn't trust banks; I didn't know who to go to. The reason I do not raise any fuss is because I have been taught not to point a finger at those not doing anything to help you, do it yourself. I just know we need more black people to share knowledge, open the door and let us in so that we can be functional and elevate to spread the word to the next person. Not every black person is broke; they are afraid to spend and invest. It's so important that when God blesses you, you bless others, don't just close your fist, and say, "Oh I got mine."

OBESITY

Obesity is something that sneaks up on you like a thief in the night. At one point, you have a great weight and feel comfortable between the ages of nineteen to twenty-five. It seems like after college, military or after high school, you start eating out and eating the wrong things, start dating, trying to find the right male or female, just having your first child, or hanging with the fellows. By the time you realize it, you have gained twenty to twenty-five pounds. It is something about the weight that seems like it pulls you toward more poor eating habits, it did for me. You don't think about the calorie intake, you just know you want something good to eat. Your friends call and encourage you "Let's go here, let's go there" and because most of us are grown and have left home, all the fast-food places have specials, all you can eat, chicken, pizza, those are the foods that catch our attention when we have our money. In our twenties and thirties, we were busy trying to furnish our house, buy a nice car. We are working and exercise is not in the forecast. I know I talked a good talk. *Girl, I must start walking, man I got to lay off the beer. I must hit the gym.* Sounds good, but we don't do anything; now we look at ourselves and another thirty pounds have caught us. I can't speak for everyone, but in my era, calories and health weren't a big subject, at my school, I don't remember health. I think it's so important that we learn about calories and food intake because nobody thinks about this early. Nobody taught us about diabetes and high blood pressure in high school. It wasn't illustrated. I believe that when we break things down, I remember eating a half gallon of ice cream and going to bed, eating a whole pizza, and going to bed. When we went to McDonalds, I had two burgers, two shakes and fries. No one ever told me that if I continued to eat, I would continue to gain weight. We thought we looked good. There are so many reasons that obesity happens:

depression, relationships, positions, jobs, time, and it's expensive to eat healthy. Before we know it, it's too late, thirty or forty pounds extra and now we don't know what to do because we are winded, shopping at the plus sized clothes. Now the social life is kicking in. The job is going well; fresh haircuts, dating or whatever now becomes the trend, followed by alcohol. Alcohol is one of the worst things to encounter other than weight. It is hard to reverse the aftereffects. Weight and alcohol have been my struggle. Finances can change quickly, living can change quickly, better cars, better relationships, from the streets to church, new friends, but it's something about weight and alcohol. Once it starts, it is almost impossible to stop and recover your losses. *Alcohol has been my best friend*, I thought. When I didn't have a friend, when I did not have church or anything, alcohol would call my name. Every day I knew my problem was getting worse. When I got to my lowest, I found out I didn't need anyone to drink with. I could drink before going to work, sit in my car and drink and figure things out. All I needed was food, snacks and alcohol. It just overtook me until I said *if I want to live, I must stop*. It took me ten years of prayer to stop drinking. It took ten years because I kept going back. I was drinking a fifth at first, then I moved to a pint, to a half pint, to little bottles and back to pints because of events like the homecoming party, a wedding, a game or a friend would come from time to time. It wasn't until two life threatening episodes that I learned mentally and physically it was time to stop. I didn't want a drink, no taste, no smell. It became so rough I knew

God wasn't playing. I found myself sitting in the car praying with my hands in the air. It's been about three months now and I sit with friends that are drinking and I don't want it. It's amazing what God can do. It's mental, you must ask God for strength and power to quit. I heard when I was younger a friend told another friend he had stopped drinking and came home from rehab. One of my uncles who was his friend said, "Let's go by some classmates, the classmates hung out behind a liquor store, under the tree. He said, "There they go, Let's not go there, they are drinking." My uncle said, "I thought you said you are free from drinking". He said, "I am". My uncle replied, "If you can't go around alcohol, how do you know you are free?" Sometimes the only way to stop is not being around alcohol, but then, are you free? I am blessed to go around with friends and not want to drink. They ask me if I want one. I just say no. I have learned you don't have to drink to have a good time. When you are around people with addictions, it can rub off on you. The scripture says, "I can do all things through Christ." I must truly say, that is the only way I became free. There have been many nights that I ask God to please take it away, laying in the bed drunk, asking God why me and before I get up and get dressed, it's calling my name.

SACRIFICE

Sacrifice is one of the hardest things to do. It's been a strong hold for me to sacrifice because we want to keep up with the Jones'. There comes a point that you must step back and realize you must let others go on. Friends say, "We going to ride tonight?"; you have to say no. Michael Jackson says that you must start with the man in the mirror. Take a chair and mirror and sit in the bathroom, tilt your head and ask yourself; *Who are you? And what's your assignment? What are you going to be in life? What impact will I make? Who am I?* Just sit don't move. It took a long time for me to realize that I had a purpose and in order to get there, I had to make sacrifices. I didn't get the push coming out of high school, I must admit. I wanted to do better; no one had to twist my arm, I knew I wanted to be special. If you ever met me, you could remember this about me. My next question was, "With no money, an education, fancy clothes, big words, what are you going to do with your life?" I made up in my mind to be a professional football player, so I studied the profession. I studied players like Mean Joe Green, Jack Lambert and teams like Pittsburg Steelers, Buffalo Bills; those were guys that had reputations of being stand up athletes. I had to study what they did, how they positioned themselves to be in shape and how they worked out harder than others. What made them great was determination. They had to be consistent. They had to study their opponent, spend a lot of time lifting weights and working out and they had to eat proper meals. While some of my friends were able to go fishing, hunting, playing, bike riding, I was jogging, lifting weights, watching professional football on Sundays and college football on Saturdays. While reading articles on these guys, I found out they were a lot like me; single parent home, low income and I looked at their situation and used my situation to know that I didn't want to raise my kids poor. I wanted them to wear nice clothes, drive nice cars and have a better start in life than I did. I wanted a nice bank account, to have choices and to travel. When I walked down the street, I wanted people to tell me about my great job. This would take a lot of sacrifice. While everyone else would be having a good time, I would be lifting weights. My friends would tell me "You are missing a good time, missing parties, you will miss championships." More partners will say you do not spend enough time with them, but it's hard when you are trying to get a career as a professional. It's hard and it may not make sense to them, but that's okay; some of your other friends will come to you and say, "You kicked us to the curb, man you are changing." My grandparents would say don't let the right hand know what the left hand is doing. I love it when I see high school or college students going to school and working. I know they are on a mission, and they are sacrificing. What a sacrifice, putting off something to better yourself. We make so many sacrifices for our children, opening bank accounts at birth, saving for college, but there is also another sacrifice that we make sometimes; working an extra job for the family to have a trip, but more important to sacrifice for your parents, serious sacrifices for parents to be taken care of. It's a major sacrifice making sure they are okay. You might have to go cook, or just go sit and listen to them. Your day or weekend can be planned for yourself and then you get a call that says Momma or Daddy fell or they need to go to the doctor. You must sacrifice for the kids, because sometimes they make mistakes. You have made mistakes and you might know what it feels like if there was never anyone to make sacrifices for you. You might have to go into your 401K. Sometimes the sacrifice is in the relationship, where you may have to put bills on hold, childhood friends may need to use your car or credit card to feed their family. Sacrifice sometimes even if you are not sure you will get your money back. Black people have been making sacrifices for so many years. We know how to sacrifice. So many times, we must make sacrifices to help others.

PROCRASTINATION

Procrastination is a blockage of the mind. Constantly talking about things that you never actually plan to do, but it sounds good. Procrastination is one major reason why we don't achieve, and a detour to accomplishing your dreams, hopes and your future. For some reason, you can't get started or don't finish. The first step seems so hard. You know how to do it, but that blockage keeps you at a standstill. It seems that it's not important enough to execute. You may say, "I'm going to get married, go back to school, get a better job, we are going somewhere for a vacation, I have to buy a new car, I'm going to do this and that." You look up and five to ten years later, the person is still saying the same thing. It's a sticky situation and people get stuck; excuses step in, kids to take care of, bills that need to be paid, you are no longer working the hours that you once did, Momma has to go to dialysis. Excuses and procrastination ride in the car together. Procrastination will cause you to lose friends because you try to avoid each other. You may see the person that you may owe and promised to pay in a restaurant and must leave the restaurant to avoid them. You know they will ask you for the money that you have been owing them for a long time and you hate to tell another lie. You can't bring your family to church because you know that you owe several people in the church. It is better to go to the person and be honest, letting them know you have fallen on harder times than when you borrowed the money, and that as soon as you can, you will do what you promised. Sometimes there are people that just won't do the right thing. You took the loan because you were in need and even when you could, you didn't pay the person you owed. Do the right thing!

YOUR WORD, YOUR HANDSHAKE

I remember a black man's word being his bond. Real black men stood on their word. They shook hands after making a deal. A firm handshake and look you in the eye and say, *you can count on me.* If you called a real black man a liar, those were guaranteed fighting words. When a real black man knew he couldn't keep his commitment, he would come by to explain what happened, whether his mother got sick, baby got sick, these things just happen. The relationship would go a lot easier. Some men still played games, but the majority could be held then to their handshake. What has happened to our Word, our handshake? I no longer see it. People have become so desperate and uncaring that they just say what they need to so that they can get what they need. They make promises that they know they have no intention of keeping. The sad thing is that sooner or later, karma will come back and bite them. They may get over on that person then, but it may come back to them ten times worse.

THE
CLOSING
MY HEART HAS FELT

MY THOUGTHS

IS IT POSSIBLE for everyone to ever get along? That I don't know. Love is a powerful statement and there is a time when we can all be on the same level, college, high school, or playing sports but, at the end of the day some Caucasian men will always think he is better than you and me when he isn't. He is a vicious human being. I've been here long enough to study the Caucasian man and I don't understand why they think so little of blacks, even with the reality that we have no different desires than they do. The one main difference is in color. As I stated earlier in this book is not about being a racist, it's about giving the Caucasian people an understanding so that they can truly learn what they are doing wrong to black people. If we are truthful about the situation some blacks are smarter, craftier, and some feel that no matter what we accomplish, it's not good enough even though we have proven ourselves over the years. The bad part is that some black people have gotten to the point they really don't care if Caucasian people like us or not. When we come in contact with Caucasian people, we feel we already know what to expect, so we have an attitude because it's been so much done in the past that we don't trust them. I've never heard anyone in my circle of friends saying they don't like Caucasians; they say I just don't fool with them at all. I've never heard women say I hate Caucasian people and what they stand for even though sometimes they had to treat their children and take care of them better than they were allowed to take care of their own children. Black women are some of the most loving and forgiving human beings there are. Most black people are not the kind to hate, we love, we will help others. Even though we have never had anything, we have always been willing to give others the shirt off our backs. We are people of respect, humbleness, love and pride. When others are hurting, we help. We lend a listening ear to a person. It ain't the conversations that black people start that keeps us from getting along. It is the things that are said to us and about us that makes the train run off the track really quick, something that is said inappropriately because so many Caucasian people still have the racist mentality and believe they can talk to you with disrespect, and you have to accept it. Some people now still are willing to lose their jobs, miss a promotion, whatever because we shouldn't have to bow down to Caucasian people and we know the more we do, the more disrespect we will get from them. I picked up a lady one day that had just been fired on the phone with a coworker. She said he is not going to talk to me like that he's going to respect me. She said she is from New York, and she moved here three months ago. She said we stand up and don't let people walk over us. She got fired for standing up and no one else would. Jim Crow is gone you can't bully us anymore we're not stepping off the sidewalk anymore to let the Caucasian person pass. We are learning to dry our tears and start fighting back. We have realized you can't make it without us anyway, you expect us to do the physical work. Not being rude, just standing up for our rights, everyone has the right to be treated like human beings like everyone else.

MY PRAYER

My prayer is that one day all races of people can get along and have love and respect for each other. We must learn how to love each other regardless of race, creed, or color, or neither will see the kingdom of heaven. We must find some common ground as men and women, meet in the middle, and say enough is enough. My prayer is that God will bless all of us who are willing to put down our axes and hammers and accept the fact that I am who I am.

MY WISH

My wish is that we can all educate each other about each other, learn about each other, and get to know each other for who we are. My wish is that all men can shake hands as strangers, shake hands, and complement each other, whether it's our suit, our car, or whatever. I wish that we can one day laugh and have fun and that there is no name-calling or retaliation because of our color. No more nigger calling; no more honkie, cracker, or jungle monkey. Please help me make this wish come true.

MY CONCLUSION

My eyes have seen many things, my ears have heard many things, and my body has endured many scars, but at fifty-five years old, this world didn't change me to be what it wanted me to be. It was a slow process because I was meant to be shut out. I had to learn to read between the lines. I learned to quit talking and listening; I found out that in this life, if you look with your eyes, you can see the clouds moving and the wind blowing; listen and hear the thunder roar. If you ask questions, people can give a warning of what lies ahead. If you comprehend this on your own, learning opens the door to wisdom and knowledge. Some mistakes are good. We must go through some things to learn. Don't stay where you are. Learn about friendships, family, jobs, and religion, just to name a few. It's there for you; just don't get distracted. Growing up in Arkansas, music was a big part of our community, and my mom played a song that says, "It takes a fool to learn that love don't love anyone." So, my meaning to all is that this is why I woke up black, confused, abused, disrespected, etc., but I'm also going to go to sleep black, proud, and with my dignity and respect. So, if you have read this book, I thank you, I hope I didn't offend anyone. This is not about race, prejudice, or anything like that. It's about waking up black, so I say to my kings and queens, stay woke. Don't go to sleep on the systems that continue to oppress you. *P.S. Thank you. I love you, and there is nothing you can do about it.*

ABOUT THE AUTHOR

MARVIN MICHAEL O'BRYANT was born on May 1, 1967, to Erma O'Bryant-Dollison, and Charles and Irene Williams. He is the youngest among his siblings, with sister Deborah Shelton English, and brothers Dwayne O'Bryant, Brian Williams, and Keith Williams. He is a native of both Little Rock, and Pine Bluff, Arkansas. Marvin takes immense pride in being a devoted father to his three children: Marvin O'Bryant, Jr., Kenneth Green, and Courtney Lee.

Throughout his educational journey, Marvin attended Oklahoma University in Miami, OK, as well as the University of Central Arkansas (UCA) and the University of Arkansas at Pine Bluff (UAPB). In terms of his professional accomplishments, Marvin holds a barber license and has amassed 30 years of experience in the field. He is the esteemed CEO and Founder of Classic Barbershop, having attained the distinguished title of Master Barber.

In addition to his thriving barber career, Marvin has ventured into various other endeavors. He has authored five books, including his latest publication, "I Woke Up Black." Furthermore, he has dug into the realm of filming projects, including the production of reality shows.

Marvin's unwavering passion for unity extends to his personal and professional life. When He's not engaged in his various pursuits, Marvin enjoys engaging in youth motivational speaking, writing, practicing meditation, and indulging in the pleasure of smoking cigars.

Marvin attributes his success and blessings to God and expresses deep gratitude for the support of his loved ones and community.